www.EffortlessMath.com

... So Much More Online!

✓ FREE Math lessons

✓ More Math learning books!

✓ Mathematics Worksheets

✓ Online Math Tutors

Need a PDF version of this book?

Send email to: info@EffortlessMath.com

5 Full-Length SSAT Middle Level Math Practice Tests

The Practice You Need to Ace the SSAT

Middle Level Math Test

By

Reza Nazari & Ava Ross

Copyright © 2018

Reza Nazari & Ava Ross

All inquiries should be addressed to:

info@effortlessMath.com

www.EffortlessMath.com

ISBN-13: 978-1-64612-103-8

ISBN-10: 1-64612-103-1

Published by: Effortless Math Education

www.EffortlessMath.com

Description

5 Full-Length SSAT Middle Level Math Practice Tests, which reflects the 2019 and 2020 test guidelines and topics, is designed to help you hone your math skills, overcome your exam anxiety, and boost your confidence -- and do your best to ace the SSAT Middle Level Math Test. The realistic and full-length SSAT Middle Level Math tests, which reflect the format and question types on the GED, show you how the test is structured and what math topics you need to master. The practice test questions are followed by answer explanations to help you find your weak areas, learn from your mistakes, and raise your SSAT Middle Level Math score.

The surest way to succeed on SSAT Middle Level Math Test is with intensive practice in every math topic tested-- and that's what you will get in *5 Full-Length SSAT Middle Level Math Practice Tests*. This SSAT Middle Level Math new edition has been updated to replicate questions appearing on the most recent SSAT Middle Level Math tests. This is a precious learning tool for SSAT Middle Level Math test takers who need extra practice in math to improve their SSAT Math score. After taking the SSAT Math practice tests in this book, you will have solid foundation and adequate practice that is necessary to succeed on the SSAT Middle Level Math test. **This book is your ticket to ace the SSAT Middle Level Math!**

5 Full-Length SSAT Middle Level Math Practice Tests contains many exciting and unique features to help you improve your test scores, including:

- Content 100% aligned with the 2019 - 2020 SSAT Middle Level test

- Written by SSAT Math tutors and test experts

- Complete coverage of all SSAT Middle Level Math concepts and topics which you will be tested

- Detailed answers and explanations for every SSAT Middle Level Math practice questions to help you learn from your mistakes

- 5 full-length practice tests (featuring new question types) with detailed answers

This SSAT Middle Level Math book and other Effortless Math Education books are used by thousands of students each year to help them review core content areas, brush-up in math, discover their strengths and weaknesses, and achieve their best scores on the SSAT Middle Level test.

About the Author

Reza Nazari is the author of more than 100 Math learning books including:
– **Math and Critical Thinking Challenges:** For the Middle and High School Student
– **GRE Math in 30 Days**
– **ASVAB Math Workbook 2018 – 2019**
– **Effortless Math Education Workbooks**
– and many more Mathematics books …

Reza is also an experienced Math instructor and a test–prep expert who has been tutoring students since 2008. Reza is the founder of Effortless Math Education, a tutoring company that has helped many students raise their standardized test scores—and attend the colleges of their dreams. Reza provides an individualized custom learning plan and the personalized attention that makes a difference in how students view math.

You can contact Reza via email at:
reza@EffortlessMath.com

Find Reza's professional profile at:
goo.gl/zoC9rJ

Contents

SSAT Middle Level Test Review

The SSAT, or Secondary School Admissions Test, is a standardized test to help determine admission to private elementary, middle and high schools.

There are currently three Levels of the SSAT:

- ✓ Lower Level (for students in 3rd and 4th grade)
- ✓ Middle Level (for students in 5th-7th grade)
- ✓ Upper Level (for students in 8th-11th grade)

There are six sections on the SSAT Middle Level Test:

- ✓ Writing: 25 minutes.
- ✓ Math section: 25 questions, 30 minutes
- ✓ Reading section: 40 questions, 40 minutes
- ✓ Verbal section: 60 questions, 30 minutes
- ✓ Math section: 25 questions, 30 minutes
- ✓ Experimental: 16 questions, 15 minutes.

In this book, there are 5 complete SSAT Middle Level Math Practice Tests. Take these tests to see what score you'll be able to receive on a real SSAT Middle Level test.

Good luck!

Time to Test

Time to refine your skill with a practice examination

Take a practice SSAT Middle Level Mathematics Test to simulate the test day experience. After you've finished, score your test using the answer keys.

Before You Start

- You'll need a pencil and a timer to take the test.

- After you've finished the test, review the answer key to see where you went wrong.

- Use the answer sheet provided to record your answers. (You can cut it out or photocopy it)

- You will receive 1 point for every correct answer, and you will lose $\frac{1}{4}$ point for each incorrect answer. There is no penalty for skipping a question.

Calculators are NOT permitted for the SSAT Middle Level Test

Good Luck!

SSAT Middle Level Math Practice Test 1

2019 - 2020

Two Parts

Total number of questions: 50

Section 1: 25 questions

Section 2: 25 questions

Total time for two parts: 60 Minutes

SSAT Middle Level Math Practice Test 1 Answer Sheet

Remove (or photocopy) this answer sheet and use it to complete the practice test.

SSAT Middle Level Mathematics Practice Test 1 Answer Sheet

SSAT Middle Level Practice Test 1 Section 1

1 (A)(B)(C)(D)(E)	11 (A)(B)(C)(D)(E)	21 (A)(B)(C)(D)(E)
2 (A)(B)(C)(D)(E)	12 (A)(B)(C)(D)(E)	22 (A)(B)(C)(D)(E)
3 (A)(B)(C)(D)(E)	13 (A)(B)(C)(D)(E)	23 (A)(B)(C)(D)(E)
4 (A)(B)(C)(D)(E)	14 (A)(B)(C)(D)(E)	24 (A)(B)(C)(D)(E)
5 (A)(B)(C)(D)(E)	15 (A)(B)(C)(D)(E)	25 (A)(B)(C)(D)(E)
6 (A)(B)(C)(D)(E)	16 (A)(B)(C)(D)(E)	
7 (A)(B)(C)(D)(E)	17 (A)(B)(C)(D)(E)	
8 (A)(B)(C)(D)(E)	18 (A)(B)(C)(D)(E)	
9 (A)(B)(C)(D)(E)	19 (A)(B)(C)(D)(E)	
10 (A)(B)(C)(D)(E)	20 (A)(B)(C)(D)(E)	

SSAT Middle Level Practice Test 1 Section 2

1 (A)(B)(C)(D)(E)	11 (A)(B)(C)(D)(E)	21 (A)(B)(C)(D)(E)
2 (A)(B)(C)(D)(E)	12 (A)(B)(C)(D)(E)	22 (A)(B)(C)(D)(E)
3 (A)(B)(C)(D)(E)	13 (A)(B)(C)(D)(E)	23 (A)(B)(C)(D)(E)
4 (A)(B)(C)(D)(E)	14 (A)(B)(C)(D)(E)	24 (A)(B)(C)(D)(E)
5 (A)(B)(C)(D)(E)	15 (A)(B)(C)(D)(E)	25 (A)(B)(C)(D)(E)
6 (A)(B)(C)(D)(E)	16 (A)(B)(C)(D)(E)	
7 (A)(B)(C)(D)(E)	17 (A)(B)(C)(D)(E)	
8 (A)(B)(C)(D)(E)	18 (A)(B)(C)(D)(E)	
9 (A)(B)(C)(D)(E)	19 (A)(B)(C)(D)(E)	
10 (A)(B)(C)(D)(E)	20 (A)(B)(C)(D)(E)	

SSAT Middle Level Math

Practice Test 1

Section 1

25 questions

Total time for this test: 30 Minutes

You may NOT use a calculator on this part.

1. If 30 percent of a number is 60, then 20 percent of the same number is ...
   (A) 12
   (B) 18
   (C) 25
   (D) 30
   (E) 40

2. Which of the following is NOT equal to 2×0.4?
   (A) 4×0.2
   (B) 1×0.8
   (C) $\frac{16}{8} \times \frac{4}{10}$
   (D) $\frac{5}{15} \times 3$
   (E) 0.8×1

3. Sara has M books. Mary has 6 more books than Sara. If Mary gives Sara 4 books, how many books will Mary have, in terms of M?
   (A) M
   (B) $M + 1$
   (C) $M + 2$
   (D) $M + 6$
   (E) $M - 6$

4. If $\frac{x}{2} = 30$, then $\frac{3x}{2} = ?$
   (A) 10
   (B) 20
   (C) 30
   (D) 45
   (E) 90

5. Which of the following is closest to $\frac{1}{6}$ of 40?
   (A) 0.3×6
   (B) 0.3×5
   (C) 0.2×30
   (D) 0.2×35
   (E) 0.2×39.5

6. What is the area of a square whose diagonal is 8?
   (A) 16
   (B) 32
   (C) 36
   (D) 64
   (E) 80

7. An angle is equal to one fifth of its supplement. What is the measure of that angle?
   (A) 20
   (B) 30
   (C) 45
   (D) 60
   (E) 150

8. A $44 shirt now selling for $28 is discounted by approximately what percent?
   (A) 20%
   (B) 36%
   (C) 40%
   (D) 60%
   (E) 80%

9. 6 liters of water are poured into an aquarium that's $25cm$ long, $5cm$ wide, and $60cm$ high. How many centimeters will the water level in the aquarium rise due to this added water?
   ($1\ liter\ of\ water = 1,000\ cm^3$)
   (A) 80
   (B) 48
   (C) 20
   (D) 10
   (E) 8

10. The perimeter of the trapezoid below is 64. What is its area?
    (A) $260\ cm^2$
    (B) $234\ cm^2$
    (C) $216\ cm^2$
    (D) $130\ cm^2$
    (E) $108cm^2$

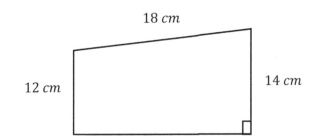

11. The score of Emma was half as that of Ava and the score of Mia was twice that of Ava. If the score of Mia was 40, what is the score of Emma?
    (A) 10
    (B) 18
    (C) 20
    (D) 30
    (E) 32

12. Two third of 9 is equal to $\frac{2}{5}$ of what number?
   (A) 60
   (B) 20
   (C) 15
   (D) 30
   (E) 36

13. If three times a number added to 5 equals to 32, what is the number?
   (A) 2
   (B) 4
   (C) 6
   (D) 9
   (E) 10

14. Solve for x: $4(x + 1) = 6(x - 4) + 20$
   (A) 12
   (B) 6.5
   (C) 4
   (D) 2
   (E) 1

15. Karen is 9 years older than her sister Michelle, and Michelle is 4 years younger than her brother David. If the sum of their ages is 82, how old is Michelle?

   (A) 14
   (B) 23
   (C) 22
   (D) 25
   (E) 30

16. Two-kilograms apple and two-kilograms orange cost $26.4. If one-kilogram apple costs $4.2 how much does one-kilogram orange cost?
   (A) $9
   (B) $6
   (C) $5.5
   (D) $5
   (E) $4.5

17. The average weight of 18 girls in a class is $50\ kg$ and the average weight of 32 boys in the same class is $62\ kg$. What is the average weight of all the 50 students in that class?
    (A) 57.68
    (B) 61.68
    (C) 61.90
    (D) 62.20
    (E) 64.00

18. What is the value of x in this equation? $6(x + 4) = 78$
    (A) 4
    (B) 6
    (C) 9
    (D) 10
    (E) 12

19. When a number is subtracted from 32 and the difference is divided by that number, the result is 3. What is the value of the number?

    (A) 2
    (B) 4
    (C) 8
    (D) 12
    (E) 15

20. Which is the correct statement?
    (A) $\frac{3}{4} > 0.8$
    (B) $10\% = \frac{2}{5}$
    (C) $3 < \frac{5}{2}$
    (D) $\frac{5}{6} > 0.8$
    (E) $2.5\% = 0.25$

21. In a group of 5 books, the average number of pages is 24. Mary adds a book with 36 pages to the group. What is the new average number of pages per book?
    (A) 20
    (B) 22
    (C) 24
    (D) 26
    (E) 30

22. A football team won exactly 70% of the games it played during last session. Which of the following could be the total number of games the team played last season?
   (A) 49
   (B) 40
   (C) 32
   (D) 12
   (E) 9

23. If a gas tank can hold 35 gallons, how many gallons does it contain when it is $\frac{2}{5}$ full?
   (A) 50
   (B) 125
   (C) 62.5
   (D) 14
   (E) 8

24. What is the value of x in the following figure? (Figure is not drawn to scale)
   (A) 150
   (B) 145
   (C) 125
   (D) 105
   (E) 85

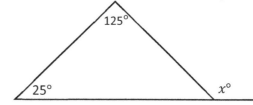

25. The capacity of a red box is 20% bigger than the capacity of a blue box. If 36 books can be put in the red box, how many books can be put in the blue box?

   (A) 15
   (B) 20
   (C) 24
   (D) 30
   (E) 32

IF YOU FINISH BEFORE TIME IS CALLED, YOU MAY CHECK YOUR WORK ON THIS SECTION ONLY. DO NOT TURN TO OTHER SECTION IN THE TEST. **STOP**

SSAT Middle Level Math

Practice Test 1

Section 2

25 questions

Total time for this test: 30 Minutes

You may NOT use a calculator on this part.

1. A taxi driver earns $8 per 1-hour work. If he works 10 hours a day and in 1 hour he uses 2-liters petrol with price $1 for 1-liter. How much money does he earn in one day?
   (A) $90
   (B) $88
   (C) $70
   (D) $60
   (E) $56

2. Which of the following is less than $\frac{1}{5}$?
   (A) $\frac{1}{4}$
   (B) 0.5
   (C) $\frac{1}{7}$
   (D) 0.28
   (E) 0.31

3. Amy and John work in a same company. Last month, both of them received a raise of 20 percent. If Amy earns $30.00 per hour now and John earns $28.80, Amy earned how much more per hour than John before their raises?
   (A) $8.25
   (B) $4.25
   (C) $3.00
   (D) $2.25
   (E) $1.00

4. Three people can paint 3 houses in 12 days. How many people are needed to paint 6 houses in 6 days?
   (A) 6
   (B) 8
   (C) 12
   (D) 16
   (E) 20

5. If $N \times (6 - 3) = 12$ then $N =$?
   (A) 4
   (B) 12
   (C) 13
   (D) 14
   (E) 18

6. The length of a rectangle is 3 times of its width. If the length is 24, what is the perimeter of the rectangle?
   (A) 24
   (B) 30
   (C) 36
   (D) 48
   (E) 64

7. In the figure below, what is the value of x? (Figure is not drawn to scale)
   (A) 43
   (B) 72
   (C) 77
   (D) 90
   (E) 98

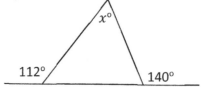

8. If $x \blacksquare y = 4x + y - 2$, what is the value of $4 \blacksquare 12$?
   (A) 4
   (B) 18
   (C) 26
   (D) 36
   (E) 48

9. The width of a rectangle is $4x$, the length is $6x$, and the perimeter of the rectangle is 90. What is the value of x?
   (A) 1
   (B) 2.2
   (C) 3
   (D) 4.5
   (E) 5.8

10. How many tiles of $8 \ cm^2$ is needed to cover a floor of dimension $7 \ cm$ by $24 \ cm$?
    (A) 6
    (B) 12
    (C) 21
    (D) 24
    (E) 30

11. If 0.65 equals $65M$, what is the value of M?
    (A) 0.10
    (B) 0.01
    (C) 1.00
    (D) 11.01
    (E) 0.11

12. If $z = 3x + 5$, what does $2z + 3$ equal?
   (A) $6x + 6$
   (B) $6x + 12$
   (C) $6x - 12$
   (D) $6x - 6$
   (E) $6x + 13$

13. If 96 is the product of 4 and $8x$, then 96 is divisible by which of the following?
   (A) $x + 4$
   (B) $2x - 1$
   (C) $5x - 3$
   (D) $x \times 3$
   (E) $3x + 1$

$$0.0ABC \qquad\qquad 0.0D$$

14. The letters represent two decimals listed above. One of the decimals is equivalent to $\dfrac{1}{16}$ and the other is equivalent to $\dfrac{1}{25}$. What is the product of C and D?
   (A) 0
   (B) 5
   (C) 25
   (D) 20
   (E) 40

15. $\dfrac{x}{x-2} = \dfrac{4}{5}$, $x - 5 =?$
   (A) -13
   (B) -15
   (C) -17
   (D) 12
   (E) 15

16. A company pays its employer $7,000 plus 3% of all sales profit. If x is the number of all sales profit, which of the following represents the employer's revenue?

   (A) $0.03x$
   (B) $0.97x - 7,000$
   (C) $0.03x + 7,000$
   (D) $0.97x + 7,000$
   (E) $0.3x + 7,000$

17. In a certain bookshelf of a library, there are 35 biology books, 85 history books, and 90 language books. What is the ratio of the number of biology books to the total number of books in this bookshelf?

(A) $\frac{1}{4}$

(B) $\frac{1}{6}$

(C) $\frac{2}{7}$

(D) $\frac{3}{8}$

(E) $\frac{1}{4}$

18. If $5,000 + A - 200 = 7,400$, then $A = \cdots$
   (A) 200
   (B) 600
   (C) 1,600
   (D) 2,600
   (E) 3,000

19. The circle graph below shows all Mr. Green's expenses for last month. If he spent \$770 on his car, how much did he spend for his rent?
   (A) \$700
   (B) \$740
   (C) \$780
   (D) \$810
   (E) \$945

Mr. Green's monthly expenses

20. If $5 \times M + 3 = 5$, M equals to ….
   (A) 2
   (B) 4
   (C) $\frac{2}{5}$
   (D) 6
   (E) $\frac{1}{3}$

21. Which of the following is equal to $\frac{52.6}{100}$?
   (A) 52.6
   (B) 5.26
   (C) 526.0
   (D) 0.0526
   (E) 0.526

22. In the following figure, point Q lies on line A, what is the value of y if $x = 28$? (Figure is not drawn to scale)
    (A) 32
    (B) 37
    (C) 42
    (D) 45
    (E) 56

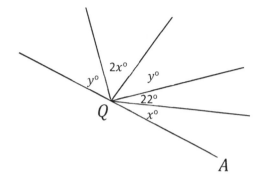

23. A container holds 2.5 gallons of water when it is $\frac{5}{24}$ full. How many gallons of water does the container hold when it's full?
    (A) 8
    (B) 12
    (C) 16
    (D) 20
    (E) 30

24. At a Zoo, the ratio of lions to tigers is 3 to 1. Which of the following could NOT be the total number of lions and tigers in the zoo?
    (A) 64
    (B) 80
    (C) 98
    (D) 104
    (E) 160

25. If x is greater than 18, then $\frac{1}{3}$ of x must be...
    (A) Greater than 3
    (B) Greater than 6
    (C) Equal to 6
    (D) Equal to 3
    (E) Less than 3

IF YOU FINISH BEFORE TIME IS CALLED, YOU MAY CHECK YOUR WORK ON THIS SECTION ONLY. DO NOT TURN TO ANY OTHER SECTION IN THE TEST. **STOP**

SSAT Middle Level Math Practice Test 2

2019 - 2020

Two Parts

Total number of questions: 50

Section 1: 25 questions

Section 2: 25 questions

Total time for two parts: 60 Minutes

SSAT Practice Test 2 Answer Sheet

Remove (or photocopy) this answer sheet and use it to complete the practice test.

SSAT Middle Level Mathematics Practice Test 2 Answer Sheet

SSAT Middle Level Practice Test 2 Section 1

1	Ⓐ Ⓑ Ⓒ Ⓓ Ⓔ	11 Ⓐ Ⓑ Ⓒ Ⓓ Ⓔ	21 Ⓐ Ⓑ Ⓒ Ⓓ Ⓔ
2	Ⓐ Ⓑ Ⓒ Ⓓ Ⓔ	12 Ⓐ Ⓑ Ⓒ Ⓓ Ⓔ	22 Ⓐ Ⓑ Ⓒ Ⓓ Ⓔ
3	Ⓐ Ⓑ Ⓒ Ⓓ Ⓔ	13 Ⓐ Ⓑ Ⓒ Ⓓ Ⓔ	23 Ⓐ Ⓑ Ⓒ Ⓓ Ⓔ
4	Ⓐ Ⓑ Ⓒ Ⓓ Ⓔ	14 Ⓐ Ⓑ Ⓒ Ⓓ Ⓔ	24 Ⓐ Ⓑ Ⓒ Ⓓ Ⓔ
5	Ⓐ Ⓑ Ⓒ Ⓓ Ⓔ	15 Ⓐ Ⓑ Ⓒ Ⓓ Ⓔ	25 Ⓐ Ⓑ Ⓒ Ⓓ Ⓔ
6	Ⓐ Ⓑ Ⓒ Ⓓ Ⓔ	16 Ⓐ Ⓑ Ⓒ Ⓓ Ⓔ	
7	Ⓐ Ⓑ Ⓒ Ⓓ Ⓔ	17 Ⓐ Ⓑ Ⓒ Ⓓ Ⓔ	
8	Ⓐ Ⓑ Ⓒ Ⓓ Ⓔ	18 Ⓐ Ⓑ Ⓒ Ⓓ Ⓔ	
9	Ⓐ Ⓑ Ⓒ Ⓓ Ⓔ	19 Ⓐ Ⓑ Ⓒ Ⓓ Ⓔ	
10	Ⓐ Ⓑ Ⓒ Ⓓ Ⓔ	20 Ⓐ Ⓑ Ⓒ Ⓓ Ⓔ	

SSAT Middle Level Practice Test 2 Section 2

1	Ⓐ Ⓑ Ⓒ Ⓓ Ⓔ	11 Ⓐ Ⓑ Ⓒ Ⓓ Ⓔ	21 Ⓐ Ⓑ Ⓒ Ⓓ Ⓔ
2	Ⓐ Ⓑ Ⓒ Ⓓ Ⓔ	12 Ⓐ Ⓑ Ⓒ Ⓓ Ⓔ	22 Ⓐ Ⓑ Ⓒ Ⓓ Ⓔ
3	Ⓐ Ⓑ Ⓒ Ⓓ Ⓔ	13 Ⓐ Ⓑ Ⓒ Ⓓ Ⓔ	23 Ⓐ Ⓑ Ⓒ Ⓓ Ⓔ
4	Ⓐ Ⓑ Ⓒ Ⓓ Ⓔ	14 Ⓐ Ⓑ Ⓒ Ⓓ Ⓔ	24 Ⓐ Ⓑ Ⓒ Ⓓ Ⓔ
5	Ⓐ Ⓑ Ⓒ Ⓓ Ⓔ	15 Ⓐ Ⓑ Ⓒ Ⓓ Ⓔ	25 Ⓐ Ⓑ Ⓒ Ⓓ Ⓔ
6	Ⓐ Ⓑ Ⓒ Ⓓ Ⓔ	16 Ⓐ Ⓑ Ⓒ Ⓓ Ⓔ	
7	Ⓐ Ⓑ Ⓒ Ⓓ Ⓔ	17 Ⓐ Ⓑ Ⓒ Ⓓ Ⓔ	
8	Ⓐ Ⓑ Ⓒ Ⓓ Ⓔ	18 Ⓐ Ⓑ Ⓒ Ⓓ Ⓔ	
9	Ⓐ Ⓑ Ⓒ Ⓓ Ⓔ	19 Ⓐ Ⓑ Ⓒ Ⓓ Ⓔ	
10	Ⓐ Ⓑ Ⓒ Ⓓ Ⓔ	20 Ⓐ Ⓑ Ⓒ Ⓓ Ⓔ	

SSAT Middle Level Math

Practice Test 2

Section 1

25 questions

Total time for this test: 30 Minutes

You may NOT use a calculator on this part.

1. How long does a 420–miles trip take moving at 65 miles per hour (mph)?
   (A) 4 *hours*
   (B) 6 *hours and* 24 *minutes*
   (C) 8 *hours and* 24 *minutes*
   (D) 8 *hours and* 30 *minutes*
   (E) 10 *hours and* 30 *minutes*

2. The marked price of a computer is D dollar. Its price decreased by 15% in January and later increased by 10% in February. What is the final price of the computer in D dollar?
   (A) 0.80 D
   (B) 0.88 D
   (C) 0.93 D
   (D) 1.20 D
   (E) 1.40 D

3. If 0.35 equals $350M$, what is the value of M?
   (A) 0.001
   (B) 0.01
   (C) 1.0
   (D) 1.01
   (E) 1.001

4. Jason borrowed $5,800 for three months at an annual rate of 5%. How much interest did Jason owe?
   (A) $45
   (B) $72.50
   (C) $120
   (D) $240
   (E) $480

5. If three times a certain number, increased by 10, is equal to 40, what is the number?
   (A) 10
   (B) 12
   (C) 18
   (D) 27
   (E) 54

6. If 30 percent of a number is 150, then 15 percent of the same number is ?
   (A) 75
   (B) 79
   (C) 80
   (D) 90
   (E) 120

7. The average of $13, 15, 20$ and x is 20. What is the value of x?
   (A) 9
   (B) 15
   (C) 18
   (D) 20
   (E) 32

8. In five successive hours, a car traveled $40 \ km, 45 \ km, 50 \ km, 35 \ km$ and $55 \ km$. In the next five hours, it traveled with an average speed of $55 \ km \ per \ hour$. Find the total distance the car traveled in 10 hours.
   (A) $425 \ km$
   (B) $450 \ km$
   (C) $475 \ km$
   (D) $500 \ km$
   (E) $1,000 \ km$

9. John has N toy cars. Jack has 6 more cars than John. If Jack gives John 3 cars, how many cars will Jack have, in terms of N?
   (A) N
   (B) $N - 1$
   (C) $N + 1$
   (D) $N + 2$
   (E) $N + 3$

10. What is the value of x in the following equation?

$$\frac{x + 4}{5} = 3$$

   (A) 2
   (B) 4
   (C) 6
   (D) 8
   (E) 11

11. The ratio of boys to girls in a school is $2 : 3$. If there are 500 students in a school, how many boys are in the school.
   (A) 540
   (B) 360
   (C) 300
   (D) 280
   (E) 200

12. Two third of 24 is equal to $\frac{2}{5}$ of what number?
   (A) 12
   (B) 20
   (C) 40
   (D) 60
   (E) 90

13. What is the cost of seven ounces of cheese at $0.96 *per pound*?
   (A) $0.42
   (B) $0.45
   (C) $0.48
   (D) $0.52
   (E) $0.64

14. If 60% of A is 30% of B, then B is what percent of A?
   (A) 3%
   (B) 30%
   (C) 200%
   (D) 300%
   (E) 900%

15. Sophia purchased a sofa for $504. The sofa is regularly priced at $600. What was the percent discount Sophia received on the sofa?
   (A) 12%
   (B) 16%
   (C) 20%
   (D) 25%
   (E) 40%

16. A bag contains 18 balls: two green, five black, eight blue, a brown, a red and one white. If 17 balls are removed from the bag at random, what is the probability that a brown ball has been removed?
   (A) $\frac{1}{9}$

   (B) $\frac{1}{18}$

   (C) $\frac{16}{17}$

   (D) $\frac{17}{18}$

   (E) $\frac{1}{2}$

17. When a number is subtracted from 28 and the difference is divided by that number, the result is 3. What is the value of the number?
    (A) 2
    (B) 4
    (C) 7
    (D) 12
    (E) 24

18. If 45% of a class are girls, and 25% of girls play tennis, approximately what percent of the class play tennis?
    (A) 11%
    (B) 15%
    (C) 20%
    (D) 40%
    (E) 80%

19. 44 students took an exam and 11 of them failed. What percent of the students passed the exam?
    (A) 20%
    (B) 40%
    (C) 60%
    (D) 75%
    (E) 90%

20. What is the value of x in the following equation?
$$3x + 10 = 67$$
    (A) 5
    (B) 7
    (C) 9
    (D) 11
    (E) 19

21. If $N \times \frac{4}{3} \times 7 = 0$, then $N =....$
    (A) 0
    (B) 1
    (C) 2
    (D) 3
    (E) 4

22. Jason left a $12.00 tip on a lunch that cost $60.00, approximately what percentage was the tip?

    (A) 2.5%
    (B) 10%
    (C) 15%
    (D) 20%
    (E) 25%

23. If 60% of a number is 6, what is the number?
    (A) 4
    (B) 8
    (C) 10
    (D) 12
    (E) 20

24. If $\frac{z}{5} = 4$, then $z + 3 =$?
    (A) 4
    (B) 5
    (C) 15
    (D) 20
    (E) 23

25. In 1999, the average worker's income increased $3,000 per year starting from $24,000 annual salary. Which equation represents income greater than average? (I= income, x = number of years after 1999)
    (A) $I > 3,000x + 24,000$
    (B) $I > -3,000x + 24,000$
    (C) $I < -3,000x + 24,000$
    (D) $I < 3,000x - 24,000$
    (E) $I < 24,000x + 24,000$

IF YOU FINISH BEFORE TIME IS CALLED, YOU MAY CHECK YOUR WORK ON THIS SECTION ONLY. DO NOT TURN TO ANY OTHER SECTION IN THE TEST. **STOP**

SSAT Middle Level Math

Practice Test 2

Section 2

25 questions

Total time for this test: 30 Minutes

You may NOT use a calculator on this part.

1. John has x dollars and he receives $150. He then buys a bicycle that costs $110. How much money does John have now?
   (A) $x + 150$
   (B) $x + 110$
   (C) $x + 40$
   (D) $x - 120$
   (E) $x - 40$

2. What is the value of x in this equation?
$$\frac{x - 3}{8} + 5 = 20$$
   (A) 131
   (B) 128
   (C) 123
   (D) 120
   (E) 115

3. Bob needs an 78% average in his writing class to pass. On his first 4 exams, he earned scores of 68%, 72%, 85%, and 90%. What is the minimum score Bob can earn on his fifth and final test to pass?
   (A) 80%,
   (B) 75%
   (C) 68%
   (D) 64%
   (E) 60%

4. The width of a rectangle is $6x$, the length is $8x$, and the perimeter is 84. What is the value of x?
   (A) 1
   (B) 2
   (C) 3
   (D) 4
   (E) 5

5. A bank is offering 3.5% simple interest on a savings account. If you deposit $8,000, how much interest will you earn in five years?
   (A) $360
   (B) $720
   (C) $1,400
   (D) $3,600
   (E) $4,800

6. If $(8 - 4) \times 4 = 8 + \square$, then $\square =$?
   (A) 5
   (B) 6
   (C) 7
   (D) 8
   (E) 9

7. Jason is 9 miles ahead of Joe running at 6.5 miles per hour and Joe is running at the speed of 8 miles per hour. How long does it take Joe to catch Jason?
   (A) 3 *hours*
   (B) 4 *hours*
   (C) 6 *hours*
   (D) 8 *hours*
   (E) 10 *hours*

8. In a classroom, there are y tables that can each seat 4 people and there are x tables that can each seat 8 people. What is the number of people that can be seated in the classroom?
   (A) $4y$
   (B) $8x$
   (C) $8x - 4y$
   (D) 13
   (E) $8x + 4y$

9. The area of a circle is 81π. What is the diameter of the circle?
   (A) 4
   (B) 8
   (C) 12
   (D) 14
   (E) 18

10. A shirt costing $300 is discounted 15%. After a month, the shirt is discounted another 15%. Which of the following expressions can be used to find the selling price of the shirt?
    (A) $(300)\,(0.70)$
    (B) $(300) - 300\,(0.30)$
    (C) $(300)(0.15) - (300)\,(0.15)$
    (D) $(300)\,(0.85)\,(0.85)$
    (E) $(300)(0.85)(0.85) - (300)\,(0.15)$

11. Four one – foot rulers can be split among how many users to leave each with $\frac{1}{3}$ of a ruler?
    (A) 4
    (B) 6
    (C) 12
    (D) 24
    (E) 48

12. The perimeter of a rectangular yard is 72 meters. What is its length if its width is twice its length?
    (A) 12 $meters$
    (B) 18 $meters$
    (C) 20 $meters$
    (D) 24 $meters$
    (E) 36 $meters$

13. What is the value of x in this equation? $2x + 10 = 48$
    (A) 19
    (B) 14
    (C) 12
    (D) 10
    (E) 6

14. The mean of 50 test scores was calculated as 86. But, it turned out that one of the scores was misread as 94 but it was 69. What is the mean?
    (A) 85.5
    (B) 85
    (C) 84.5
    (D) 83.5
    (E) 80.5

15. The average of 6 numbers is 15. The average of 4 of those numbers is 10. What is the average of the other two numbers?
    (A) 10
    (B) 12
    (C) 14
    (D) 15
    (E) 25

16. If $x + 5 = 8, 2y - 1 = 5$ then $xy + 15 =$
    (A) 10
    (B) 19
    (C) 24
    (D) 27
    (E) 32

17. A card is drawn at random from a standard 52–card deck, what is the probability that the card is of Hearts? (The deck includes 13 of each suit clubs, diamonds, hearts, and spades)

(A) $\frac{1}{3}$

(B) $\frac{1}{4}$

(C) $\frac{1}{6}$

(D) $\frac{1}{52}$

(E) $\frac{1}{104}$

18. Which of the following is NOT less than $\frac{1}{5}$?

(A) $\frac{1}{8}$

(B) $\frac{1}{3}$

(C) $\frac{1}{9}$

(D) 0.14

(E) 17%

19. Mr. Jones saves \$2,500 out of his monthly family income of \$65,000. What fractional part of his income does he save?

(A) $\frac{1}{26}$

(B) $\frac{1}{11}$

(C) $\frac{3}{25}$

(D) $\frac{2}{15}$

(E) $\frac{1}{15}$

20. If $5x - 6 = 39$, then $3x + 6 =$?

(A) 18

(B) 20

(C) 22

(D) 33

(E) 36

21. In two successive years, the population of a town is increased by 10% and 20%. What percent of the population is increased after two years?

(A) 32%

(B) 31%

(C) 30%

(D) 28%

(E) 22%

22. If 150% of a number is 75, then what is the 80% of that number?
    (A) 40
    (B) 50
    (C) 70
    (D) 85
    (E) 90

23. What is the equivalent temperature of $140°F$ in Celsius? ($C = Celsius$)
$$C = \frac{5}{9}(F - 32)$$
    (A) 32
    (B) 40
    (C) 48
    (D) 52
    (E) 60

24. The perimeter of the trapezoid below is $50 \ cm$. What is its area?

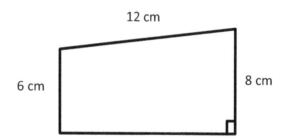

    (A) $48 \ cm^2$
    (B) $70 \ cm^2$
    (C) $168 \ cm^2$
    (D) $576 \ cm^2$
    (E) $986 \ cm^2$

25. The width of a box is one third of its length. The height of the box is half of its width. If the length of the box is $24 \ cm$, what is the volume of the box?
    (A) $81 \ cm^3$
    (B) $162 \ cm^3$
    (C) $243 \ cm^3$
    (D) $768 \ \ cm^3$
    (E) $1880 \ \ cm^3$

IF YOU FINISH BEFORE TIME IS CALLED, YOU MAY CHECK YOUR WORK ON THIS SECTION ONLY. DO NOT TURN TO OTHER SECTION IN THE TEST.

STOP

SSAT Middle Level Math Practice Test 3

2019 - 2020

Two Parts

Total number of questions: 50

Section 1: 25 questions

Section 2: 25 questions

Total time for two parts: 60 Minutes

SSAT Practice Test 3 Answer Sheet

Remove (or photocopy) this answer sheet and use it to complete the practice test.

SSAT Middle Level Mathematics Practice Test 3 Answer Sheet

SSAT Middle Level Practice Test 3 Section 1

1	Ⓐ Ⓑ Ⓒ Ⓓ Ⓔ	11	Ⓐ Ⓑ Ⓒ Ⓓ Ⓔ	21	Ⓐ Ⓑ Ⓒ Ⓓ Ⓔ
2	Ⓐ Ⓑ Ⓒ Ⓓ Ⓔ	12	Ⓐ Ⓑ Ⓒ Ⓓ Ⓔ	22	Ⓐ Ⓑ Ⓒ Ⓓ Ⓔ
3	Ⓐ Ⓑ Ⓒ Ⓓ Ⓔ	13	Ⓐ Ⓑ Ⓒ Ⓓ Ⓔ	23	Ⓐ Ⓑ Ⓒ Ⓓ Ⓔ
4	Ⓐ Ⓑ Ⓒ Ⓓ Ⓔ	14	Ⓐ Ⓑ Ⓒ Ⓓ Ⓔ	24	Ⓐ Ⓑ Ⓒ Ⓓ Ⓔ
5	Ⓐ Ⓑ Ⓒ Ⓓ Ⓔ	15	Ⓐ Ⓑ Ⓒ Ⓓ Ⓔ	25	Ⓐ Ⓑ Ⓒ Ⓓ Ⓔ
6	Ⓐ Ⓑ Ⓒ Ⓓ Ⓔ	16	Ⓐ Ⓑ Ⓒ Ⓓ Ⓔ		
7	Ⓐ Ⓑ Ⓒ Ⓓ Ⓔ	17	Ⓐ Ⓑ Ⓒ Ⓓ Ⓔ		
8	Ⓐ Ⓑ Ⓒ Ⓓ Ⓔ	18	Ⓐ Ⓑ Ⓒ Ⓓ Ⓔ		
9	Ⓐ Ⓑ Ⓒ Ⓓ Ⓔ	19	Ⓐ Ⓑ Ⓒ Ⓓ Ⓔ		
10	Ⓐ Ⓑ Ⓒ Ⓓ Ⓔ	20	Ⓐ Ⓑ Ⓒ Ⓓ Ⓔ		

SSAT Middle Level Practice Test 3 Section 2

1	Ⓐ Ⓑ Ⓒ Ⓓ Ⓔ	11	Ⓐ Ⓑ Ⓒ Ⓓ Ⓔ	21	Ⓐ Ⓑ Ⓒ Ⓓ Ⓔ
2	Ⓐ Ⓑ Ⓒ Ⓓ Ⓔ	12	Ⓐ Ⓑ Ⓒ Ⓓ Ⓔ	22	Ⓐ Ⓑ Ⓒ Ⓓ Ⓔ
3	Ⓐ Ⓑ Ⓒ Ⓓ Ⓔ	13	Ⓐ Ⓑ Ⓒ Ⓓ Ⓔ	23	Ⓐ Ⓑ Ⓒ Ⓓ Ⓔ
4	Ⓐ Ⓑ Ⓒ Ⓓ Ⓔ	14	Ⓐ Ⓑ Ⓒ Ⓓ Ⓔ	24	Ⓐ Ⓑ Ⓒ Ⓓ Ⓔ
5	Ⓐ Ⓑ Ⓒ Ⓓ Ⓔ	15	Ⓐ Ⓑ Ⓒ Ⓓ Ⓔ	25	Ⓐ Ⓑ Ⓒ Ⓓ Ⓔ
6	Ⓐ Ⓑ Ⓒ Ⓓ Ⓔ	16	Ⓐ Ⓑ Ⓒ Ⓓ Ⓔ		
7	Ⓐ Ⓑ Ⓒ Ⓓ Ⓔ	17	Ⓐ Ⓑ Ⓒ Ⓓ Ⓔ		
8	Ⓐ Ⓑ Ⓒ Ⓓ Ⓔ	18	Ⓐ Ⓑ Ⓒ Ⓓ Ⓔ		
9	Ⓐ Ⓑ Ⓒ Ⓓ Ⓔ	19	Ⓐ Ⓑ Ⓒ Ⓓ Ⓔ		
10	Ⓐ Ⓑ Ⓒ Ⓓ Ⓔ	20	Ⓐ Ⓑ Ⓒ Ⓓ Ⓔ		

SSAT Middle Level Math

Practice Test 3

Section 1

25 questions

Total time for this test: 30 Minutes

You may NOT use a calculator on this part.

1. If 30 percent of a number is 180, then 12 percent of the same number is
   (A) 60
   (B) 72
   (C) 80
   (D) 90
   (E) 120

2. If 0.45 equals $4.5F$, what is the value of $10F$?
   (A) 0.01
   (B) 0.1
   (C) 1.0
   (D) 1.01
   (E) 1.001

3. Nicole borrowed $5,800 for three months at an annual rate of 4%. How much interest did Nicole owe?
   (A) $45
   (B) $58
   (C) $116
   (D) $232
   (E) $480

4. If three times a certain number, increased by 6, is equal to 30, what is the number?
   (A) 8
   (B) 12
   (C) 20
   (D) 28
   (E) 54

5. How long does a 320–miles trip take moving at 50 miles per hour (mph)?
   (A) 6 *hours*
   (B) 6 *hours and* 24 *minutes*
   (C) 6 *hours and* 44 *minutes*
   (D) 7 *hours and* 34 *minutes*
   (E) 10 *hours and* 24 *minutes*

6. The marked price of a computer is D dollar. Its price decreased by 15% in January and later increased by 15% in February. What is the final price of the computer in D dollar?
   (A) 0.80 D
   (B) 0.88 D
   (C) 0.97 D
   (D) 1.20 D
   (E) 1.40 D

7. The average of $14, 16, 21$ and x is 20. What is the value of x?
   (A) 10
   (B) 16
   (C) 18
   (D) 20
   (E) 29

8. What is the value of x in the following equation?

$$\frac{x+4}{2} = 6$$

   (A) 2
   (B) 4
   (C) 8
   (D) 9
   (E) 10

9. John has M toy cars. Jack has 5 more cars than John. If Jack gives John 2 cars, how many cars will Jack have, in terms of M?
   (A) M
   (B) $M - 1$
   (C) $M + 1$
   (D) $M + 3$
   (E) $M + 4$

10. If 12% of A is 3% of B, then B is what percent of A?
    (A) 3%
    (B) 30%
    (C) 200%
    (D) 300%
    (E) 400%

11. The ratio of boys to girls in a school is $3 : 2$. If there are 600 students in a school, how many boys are in the school.
    (A) 540
    (B) 450
    (C) 360
    (D) 290
    (E) 240

12. In five successive hours, a car traveled 41 km, 46 km, 52 km, 36 km and 51 km. In the next five hours, it traveled with an average speed of 60 $km\ per\ hour$. Find the total distance the car traveled in 10 hours.
   (A) 420 km
   (B) 456 km
   (C) 475 km
   (D) 526 km
   (E) 1,000 km

13. Two third of 45 is equal to $\frac{4}{5}$ of what number?
   (A) 25
   (B) 37.5
   (C) 40
   (D) 42.5
   (E) 450

14. What is the cost of six ounces of cheese at $0.80 $per\ pound$?
   (A) $0.30
   (B) $0.44
   (C) $0.48
   (D) $0.52
   (E) $0.87

15. If 30% of a class are girls, and 20% of girls play tennis, what percent of the class play tennis?
   (A) 6%
   (B) 10%
   (C) 15%
   (D) 30%
   (E) 40%

16. Sophia purchased a sofa for $414.00. The sofa is regularly priced at $600.00. What was the percent discount Sophia received on the sofa?
   (A) 12%
   (B) 15%
   (C) 20%
   (D) 25%
   (E) 31%

17. When a number is subtracted from 36 and the difference is divided by that number, the result is 3. What is the value of the number?
    (A) 3
    (B) 4
    (C) 9
    (D) 12
    (E) 25

18. 50 students took an exam and 12 of them failed. What percent of the students passed the exam?
    (A) 30%
    (B) 40%
    (C) 76%
    (D) 80%
    (E) 90%

19. What is the value of x in the following equation?
$$3x + 10 = 46$$

    (A) 4
    (B) 7
    (C) 10
    (D) 11
    (E) 12

20. A bag contains 19 balls: three green, five black, eight blue, a brown, a red and one white. If 18 balls are removed from the bag at random, what is the probability that a brown ball has been removed?
    (A) $\frac{1}{9}$
    (B) $\frac{1}{7}$
    (C) $\frac{16}{19}$
    (D) $\frac{18}{19}$
    (E) $\frac{1}{2}$

21. If $M \times \frac{4}{3} \times 4 = 1$, then $M =$....
    (A) $\frac{3}{16}$
    (B) $\frac{4}{16}$
    (C) 1
    (D) 1.2
    (E) 4

22. Ava left a $4.50 tip on a lunch that cost $30.00, approximately what percentage was the tip?

    (A) 25%
    (B) 22%
    (C) 20%
    (D) 18%
    (E) 15%

23. In 1989, the average worker's income increased $3,000 per year starting from $25,000 annual salary. Which equation represents income greater than average? (I = income, x = number of years after 1989)
    (A) $I > 3,000x + 25,000$
    (B) $I > -3,000x + 25,000$
    (C) $I < -3,000x + 25,000$
    (D) $I < 3,000x - 25,000$
    (E) $I < 25,000x + 25,000$

24. If 50% of a number is 5, what is the number?
    (A) 4
    (B) 8
    (C) 10
    (D) 20
    (E) 25

25. If $\frac{z}{5} = 4$, then $z + 5 = ?$
    (A) 4
    (B) 5
    (C) 15
    (D) 20
    (E) 25

IF YOU FINISH BEFORE TIME IS CALLED, YOU MAY CHECK YOUR WORK ON THIS SECTION ONLY. DO NOT TURN TO ANY OTHER SECTION IN THE TEST. **STOP**

SSAT Middle Level Math

Practice Test 3

Section 2

25 questions

Total time for this test: 30 Minutes

You may NOT use a calculator on this part.

1. If $(10 - 5) \times 4 = 10 + \square$, then $\square = ?$

(A) 4

(B) 5

(C) 7

(D) 8

(E) 10

2. What is the value of x in this equation?

$$\frac{x - 3}{5} + 5 = 20$$

(A) 131

(B) 128

(C) 115

(D) 100

(E) 78

3. A bank is offering 5.5% simple interest on a savings account. If you deposit $7,000, how much interest will you earn in five years?

(A) $360

(B) $720

(C) $1,925

(D) $2,600

(E) $4,800

4. Emma needs an 75% average in her writing class to pass. On her first 4 exams, she earned scores of 68%, 75%, 80%, and 90%. What is the minimum score Emma can earn on her fifth and final test to pass?

(A) 70%,

(B) 62%

(C) 55%

(D) 50%

(E) 42%

5. The width of a rectangle is $4x$, its length is $6x$, and its perimeter is 40. What is the value of x?

(A) 1

(B) 2

(C) 4

(D) 5

(E) 6

6. In a classroom, there are y tables that can each seat 4 people and there are x tables that can each seat 7 people. What is the number of people that can be seated in the classroom?
   (A) $4y$
   (B) $7x$
   (C) $7x - 4y$
   (D) 13
   (E) $7x + 4y$

7. John has x dollars and he receives $150. He then buys a bicycle that costs $130. How much money does John have now?
   (A) $x + 150$
   (B) $x + 130$
   (C) $x + 20$
   (D) $x - 130$
   (E) $x - 20$

8. Jason is 15 miles ahead of Joe running at 5.5 miles per hour and Joe is running at the speed of 7 miles per hour. How long does it take Joe to catch Jason?
   (A) $3\ hours$
   (B) $4\ hours$
   (C) $6\ hours$
   (D) $8\ hours$
   (E) $10\ hours$

9. Five one – foot rulers can be split among how many users to leave each with $\frac{1}{5}$ of a ruler?
   (A) 4
   (B) 8
   (C) 25
   (D) 28
   (E) 30

10. The area of a circle is 49π. What is the diameter of the circle?
    (A) 4
    (B) 6
    (C) 12
    (D) 14
    (E) 16

11. The perimeter of a rectangular yard is 120 meters. What is its length if its width is twice its length?
    (A) 5 meters
    (B) 10 meters
    (C) 20 meters
    (D) 24 meters
    (E) 36 meters

12. A shirt costing $300 is discounted 20%. After a month, the shirt is discounted another 15%. Which of the following expressions can be used to find the selling price of the shirt?
    (A) $(300)(0.70)$
    (B) $(300) - 300(0.30)$
    (C) $(300)(0.20) - (300)(0.15)$
    (D) $(300)(0.80)(0.85)$
    (E) $(300)(0.80)(0.85) - (300)(0.15)$

13. The average of 6 numbers is 14. The average of 4 of those numbers is 10. What is the average of the other two numbers?
    (A) 10
    (B) 12
    (C) 14
    (D) 22
    (E) 28

14. What is the value of x in this equation? $3x + 10 = 37$
    (A) 18
    (B) 16
    (C) 12
    (D) 9
    (E) 6

15. If $x + 4 = 8$, $2y - 3 = 5$ then $xy + 10 =$
    (A) 9
    (B) 19
    (C) 21
    (D) 26
    (E) 32

16. A card is drawn at random from a standard 52–card deck, what is the probability that the card is of Spades? (The deck includes 13 of each suit clubs, diamonds, hearts, and spades)

    (A) $\frac{1}{4}$

    (B) $\frac{1}{2}$

    (C) $\frac{1}{6}$

    (D) $\frac{1}{78}$

    (E) $\frac{1}{104}$

17. Which of the following is NOT less than $\frac{1}{5}$?

    (A) $\frac{1}{7}$

    (B) $\frac{1}{4}$

    (C) $\frac{1}{9}$

    (D) 10%

    (E) 0.18

18. Mr. Jones saves $2,500 out of his monthly family income of $75,000. What fractional part of his income does he save?

    (A) $\frac{1}{30}$

    (B) $\frac{1}{11}$

    (C) $\frac{3}{26}$

    (D) $\frac{4}{15}$

    (E) $\frac{1}{15}$

19. The mean of 50 test scores was calculated as 90. But it turned out that one of the scores was misread as 84 but it was 59. What is the mean?

    (A) 85

    (B) 88

    (C) 89.5

    (D) 90.2

    (E) 90.5

20. If $3x - 5 = 19$, then $2x + 6 =$?

    (A) 16

    (B) 20

    (C) 22

    (D) 24

    (E) 28

21. What is the equivalent temperature of $167°F$ in Celsius? ($C = Celsius$)
$$C = \frac{5}{9}(F - 32)$$
   (A) 32
   (B) 40
   (C) 48
   (D) 52
   (E) 75

22. The width of a box is one third of its length. The height of the box is half of its width. If the length of the box is $36cm$, what is the volume of the box?
   (A) $81\ cm^3$
   (B) $165cm^3$
   (C) $248\ cm^3$
   (D) $768\ cm^3$
   (E) $2,592\ cm^3$

23. If 150% of a number is 45, then what is the 80% of that number?
   (A) 24
   (B) 45
   (C) 50
   (D) 85
   (E) 80

24. The perimeter of the trapezoid below is $46\ cm$. What is its area?
   (A) $48\ cm^2$
   (B) $70\ cm^2$
   (C) $132\ cm^2$
   (D) $576\ cm^2$
   (E) $986\ cm^2$

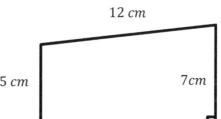

25. In two successive years, the population of a town is increased by 16% and 20%. What percent of the population is increased after two years?
   (A) 32%
   (B) 36%
   (C) 39%
   (D) 68%
   (E) 72%

IF YOU FINISH BEFORE TIME IS CALLED, YOU MAY CHECK YOUR WORK ON THIS SECTION ONLY. DO NOT TURN TO OTHER SECTION IN THE TEST. **STOP**

SSAT Middle Level Math Practice Test 4

2019 - 2020

Two Parts

Total number of questions: 50

Section 1: 25 questions

Section 2: 25 questions

Total time for two parts: 60 Minutes

SSAT Practice Test 4 Answer Sheet

Remove (or photocopy) this answer sheet and use it to complete the practice test.

SSAT Middle Level Mathematics Practice Test 4 Answer Sheet

SSAT Middle Level Practice Test 4 Section 1

1 Ⓐ Ⓑ Ⓒ Ⓓ Ⓔ	11 Ⓐ Ⓑ Ⓒ Ⓓ Ⓔ	21 Ⓐ Ⓑ Ⓒ Ⓓ Ⓔ
2 Ⓐ Ⓑ Ⓒ Ⓓ Ⓔ	12 Ⓐ Ⓑ Ⓒ Ⓓ Ⓔ	22 Ⓐ Ⓑ Ⓒ Ⓓ Ⓔ
3 Ⓐ Ⓑ Ⓒ Ⓓ Ⓔ	13 Ⓐ Ⓑ Ⓒ Ⓓ Ⓔ	23 Ⓐ Ⓑ Ⓒ Ⓓ Ⓔ
4 Ⓐ Ⓑ Ⓒ Ⓓ Ⓔ	14 Ⓐ Ⓑ Ⓒ Ⓓ Ⓔ	24 Ⓐ Ⓑ Ⓒ Ⓓ Ⓔ
5 Ⓐ Ⓑ Ⓒ Ⓓ Ⓔ	15 Ⓐ Ⓑ Ⓒ Ⓓ Ⓔ	25 Ⓐ Ⓑ Ⓒ Ⓓ Ⓔ
6 Ⓐ Ⓑ Ⓒ Ⓓ Ⓔ	16 Ⓐ Ⓑ Ⓒ Ⓓ Ⓔ	
7 Ⓐ Ⓑ Ⓒ Ⓓ Ⓔ	17 Ⓐ Ⓑ Ⓒ Ⓓ Ⓔ	
8 Ⓐ Ⓑ Ⓒ Ⓓ Ⓔ	18 Ⓐ Ⓑ Ⓒ Ⓓ Ⓔ	
9 Ⓐ Ⓑ Ⓒ Ⓓ Ⓔ	19 Ⓐ Ⓑ Ⓒ Ⓓ Ⓔ	
10 Ⓐ Ⓑ Ⓒ Ⓓ Ⓔ	20 Ⓐ Ⓑ Ⓒ Ⓓ Ⓔ	

SSAT Middle Level Practice Test 4 Section 2

1 Ⓐ Ⓑ Ⓒ Ⓓ Ⓔ	11 Ⓐ Ⓑ Ⓒ Ⓓ Ⓔ	21 Ⓐ Ⓑ Ⓒ Ⓓ Ⓔ
2 Ⓐ Ⓑ Ⓒ Ⓓ Ⓔ	12 Ⓐ Ⓑ Ⓒ Ⓓ Ⓔ	22 Ⓐ Ⓑ Ⓒ Ⓓ Ⓔ
3 Ⓐ Ⓑ Ⓒ Ⓓ Ⓔ	13 Ⓐ Ⓑ Ⓒ Ⓓ Ⓔ	23 Ⓐ Ⓑ Ⓒ Ⓓ Ⓔ
4 Ⓐ Ⓑ Ⓒ Ⓓ Ⓔ	14 Ⓐ Ⓑ Ⓒ Ⓓ Ⓔ	24 Ⓐ Ⓑ Ⓒ Ⓓ Ⓔ
5 Ⓐ Ⓑ Ⓒ Ⓓ Ⓔ	15 Ⓐ Ⓑ Ⓒ Ⓓ Ⓔ	25 Ⓐ Ⓑ Ⓒ Ⓓ Ⓔ
6 Ⓐ Ⓑ Ⓒ Ⓓ Ⓔ	16 Ⓐ Ⓑ Ⓒ Ⓓ Ⓔ	
7 Ⓐ Ⓑ Ⓒ Ⓓ Ⓔ	17 Ⓐ Ⓑ Ⓒ Ⓓ Ⓔ	
8 Ⓐ Ⓑ Ⓒ Ⓓ Ⓔ	18 Ⓐ Ⓑ Ⓒ Ⓓ Ⓔ	
9 Ⓐ Ⓑ Ⓒ Ⓓ Ⓔ	19 Ⓐ Ⓑ Ⓒ Ⓓ Ⓔ	
10 Ⓐ Ⓑ Ⓒ Ⓓ Ⓔ	20 Ⓐ Ⓑ Ⓒ Ⓓ Ⓔ	

SSAT Middle Level Math

Practice Test 4

Section 1

25 questions

Total time for this test: 30 Minutes

You may NOT use a calculator on this part.

1. If 15 percent of a number is 60, then 25 percent of the same number is ...
   (A) 65
   (B) 70
   (C) 80
   (D) 100
   (E) 120

2. Which of the following is NOT equal to 0.2×4?
   (A) 0.4×2
   (B) 1×0.8
   (C) $\frac{16}{8} \times \frac{4}{10}$
   (D) $\frac{5}{15} \times 3$
   (E) 0.8×1

3. Sara has N books. Mary has 5 more books than Sara. If Mary gives Sara 4 books, how many books will Mary have, in terms of N?
   (A) N
   (B) $N + 1$
   (C) $N + 2$
   (D) $N + 5$
   (E) $N - 5$

4. If $\frac{3x}{2} = 30$, then $\frac{2x}{5}$=?
   (A) 8
   (B) 10
   (C) 15
   (D) 20
   (E) 40

5. Which of the following is closest to $\frac{1}{5}$ of 40?
   (A) 0.3×6
   (B) 0.3×5
   (C) 0.2×30
   (D) 0.2×35
   (E) 0.2×39.5

6. What is the area of a square whose diagonal is 6?
   (A) 18
   (B) 24
   (C) 36
   (D) 60
   (E) 64

7. An angle is equal to one eighth of its supplement. What is the measure of that angle?
   (A) 15
   (B) 20
   (C) 30
   (D) 45
   (E) 160

8. A $40 shirt now selling for $28 is discounted by what percent?
   (A) 20%
   (B) 30%
   (C) 40%
   (D) 60%
   (E) 80%

9. What is the value of x in the following figure? (Figure is not drawn to scale)
   (A) 150
   (B) 145
   (C) 125
   (D) 105
   (E) 85

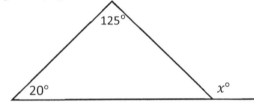

10. The perimeter of the trapezoid below is 54. What is its area?
    (A) $252cm^2$
    (B) $234\ cm^2$
    (C) $216\ cm^2$
    (D) $130\ cm^2$
    (E) $108\ cm^2$

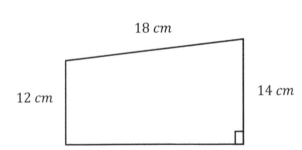

11. The score of Emma was half as that of Ava and the score of Mia was twice that of Ava. If the score of Mia was 60, what is the score of Emma?
    (A) 15
    (B) 18
    (C) 20
    (D) 30
    (E) 32

12. Two third of 30 is equal to $\frac{2}{5}$ of what number?
   (A) 15
   (B) 20
   (C) 30
   (D) 50
   (E) 60

13. If three times a number added to 6 equals to 30, what is the number?
   (A) 2
   (B) 4
   (C) 6
   (D) 8
   (E) 10

14. Solve for x: $4(x + 2) = 6(x - 4) + 20$
   (A) 12
   (B) 6
   (C) 5.5
   (D) 4
   (E) 2

15. Five years ago, Amy was three times as old as Mike was. If Mike is 10 years old now, how old is Amy?

   (A) 4
   (B) 8
   (C) 12
   (D) 15
   (E) 20

16. Two-kilograms apple and three-kilograms orange cost $26.4. If one-kilogram apple costs $4.2 how much does one-kilogram orange cost?
   (A) $9
   (B) $6
   (C) $5.5
   (D) $5
   (E) $4.5

17. The average weight of 18 girls in a class is $60 \, kg$ and the average weight of 32 boys in the same class is $62 \, kg$. What is the average weight of all the 50 students in that class?
   (A) 61.28
   (B) 61.68
   (C) 61.90
   (D) 62.20
   (E) 64.00

18. What is the value of x in this equation? $6(x + 4) = 72$
    (A) 4
    (B) 6
    (C) 8
    (D) 10
    (E) 12

19. When a number is subtracted from 20 and the difference is divided by that number, the result is 3. What is the value of the number?

    (A) 2

    (B) 4

    (C) 5

    (D) 12

    (E) 15

20. Which of the following is the correct statement?
    (A) $\frac{3}{4} > 0.8$
    (B) $10\% = \frac{2}{5}$
    (C) $3 < \frac{5}{2}$
    (D) $\frac{5}{6} > 0.8$
    (E) $2.5\% = 0.25$

21. In a group of 5 books, the average number of pages is 24. Mary adds a book with 30 pages to the group. What is the new average number of pages per book?
    (A) 20
    (B) 22
    (C) 24
    (D) 25
    (E) 30

22. A football team won exactly 80% of the games it played during last session. Which of the following could be the total number of games the team played last season?
    (A) 49
    (B) 35
    (C) 32
    (D) 12
    (E) 8

23. If a gas tank can hold 25 gallons, how many gallons does it contain when it is $\frac{2}{5}$ full?
   (A) 50
   (B) 125
   (C) 62.5
   (D) 10
   (E) 8

24. A red box is 20% greater than a blue box. If 30 books exist in the red box, how many books are in the blue box?

   (A) 9

   (B) 15

   (C) 20

   (D) 25

   (E) 26

25. 6 liters of water are poured into an aquarium that's 15 cm long, 5 cm wide, and 90 cm high. How many cm will the water level in the aquarium rise due to this added water? (1 $liter\ of\ water = 1,000\ cm^3$)
   (A) 80
   (B) 40
   (C) 20
   (D) 10
   (E) 8

IF YOU FINISH BEFORE TIME IS CALLED, YOU MAY CHECK YOUR WORK ON THIS SECTION ONLY. DO NOT TURN TO OTHER SECTION IN THE TEST. **STOP**

SSAT Middle Level Mathematics
Practice Test 4

Section 2

25 questions

Total time for this test: 30 Minutes

You may NOT use a calculator for this test.

1. A taxi driver earns $9 per 1-hour work. If he works 10 hours a day and in 1 hour he uses 2-liters petrol with price $1 for 1-liter. How much money does he earn in one day?
   (A) $90
   (B) $88
   (C) $70
   (D) $60
   (E) $56

2. Which of the following is less than $\frac{1}{5}$?
   (A) $\frac{1}{4}$
   (B) 0.5
   (C) $\frac{1}{6}$
   (D) 0.25
   (E) 0.3

3. Amy and John work in a same company. Last month, both of them received a raise of 20 percent. If Amy earns $30.00 *per hour* now and John earns $26.40, Amy earned how much more per hour than John before their raises?
   (A) $8.25
   (B) $4.25
   (C) $3.00
   (D) $2.25
   (E) $1.75

4. Four people can paint 4 houses in 10 days. How many people are needed to paint 8 houses in 5 days?
   (A) 6
   (B) 8
   (C) 12
   (D) 16
   (E) 20

5. If $N \times (5 - 3) = 12$ then $N =$?
   (A) 6
   (B) 12
   (C) 13
   (D) 14
   (E) 18

6. The length of a rectangle is 3 times of its width. If the length is 18, what is the perimeter of the rectangle?
    (A) 24
    (B) 30
    (C) 36
    (D) 48
    (E) 56

7. In the figure below, what is the value of x? (Figure is not drawn to scale)

    (A) 43
    (B) 67
    (C) 77
    (D) 90
    (E) 98

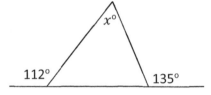

8. If $x \blacksquare y = 3x + y - 2$, what is the value of $4 \blacksquare 12$?
    (A) 4
    (B) 18
    (C) 22
    (D) 36
    (E) 48

9. The width of a rectangle is $4x$. the length is $6x$, and the perimeter of the rectangle is 80. What is the value of x?
    (A) 1
    (B) 2
    (C) 3
    (D) 4
    (E) 5

10. How many tiles of $8\ cm^2$ is needed to cover a floor of dimension $6\ cm$ by $24\ cm$?
    (A) 6
    (B) 12
    (C) 18
    (D) 24
    (E) 30

11. If 0.45 equals $450M$, what is the value of M?
    (A) 0.0001
    (B) 0.001
    (C) 0.01
    (D) 1.00
    (E) 0.11

12. If $z = 3x + 6$, what does $2z + 3$ equal?
   (A) $6x + 6$
   (B) $6x + 12$
   (C) $6x - 12$
   (D) $6x - 6$
   (E) $6x + 15$

13. If 20 is the product of 2 and $2x$, then 20 is divisible by which of the following?
   (A) $x + 4$
   (B) $2x - 4$
   (C) $x - 2$
   (D) $x \times 4$
   (E) $x + 1$

$$0.\,ABC \qquad\qquad 0.0D$$

14. The letters represent two decimals listed above. One of the decimals is equivalent to $\frac{1}{8}$ and the other is equivalent to $\frac{1}{20}$. What is the product of C and D?
   (A) 0
   (B) 5
   (C) 25
   (D) 20
   (E) 40

15. $\dfrac{x}{x-3} = \dfrac{4}{5}$, $x - 5 =$?
   (A) -12
   (B) -15
   (C) -17
   (D) 12
   (E) 15

16. A company pays its employee $4,000 plus 2% of all sales profit. If x is the number of all sales profit, which of the following represents the employer's revenue?

   (A) $0.02x$
   (B) $0.98x - 4,000$
   (C) $0.02x + 4,000$
   (D) $0.98x + 4,000$
   (E) $0.2x + 4,000$

17. In a certain bookshelf of a library, there are 35 biology books, 95 history books, and 80 language books. What is the ratio of the number of biology books to the total number of books in this bookshelf?

    (A) $\frac{1}{4}$

    (B) $\frac{1}{6}$

    (C) $\frac{2}{7}$

    (D) $\frac{3}{8}$

    (E) $\frac{1}{4}$

18. If $6,000 + A - 200 = 7,400$, then $A = \cdots$
    (A) 200
    (B) 600
    (C) 1,600
    (D) 2,200
    (E) 3,000

19. The circle graph below shows all Mr. Taylor's expenses for last month. If he spent $660 on his car, how much did he spend for his rent?

    (A) $700
    (B) $740
    (C) $780
    (D) $810
    (E) $900

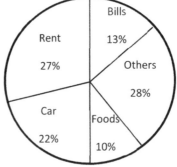

Mr. Green's monthly expenses

20. If $5 \times M + 4 = 5$, M equals to ....
    (A) 2
    (B) 4
    (C) $\frac{1}{5}$
    (D) 6
    (E) $\frac{1}{3}$

21. Which of the following is equal to $\frac{42.6}{100}$?
    (A) 42.6
    (B) 4.26
    (C) 426.0
    (D) 0.0426
    (E) 0.426

22. In the following figure, point Q lies on line n, what is the value of y if $x = 35$? (Figure is not drawn to scale)
    (A) 15
    (B) 25
    (C) 35
    (D) 45
    (E) 60

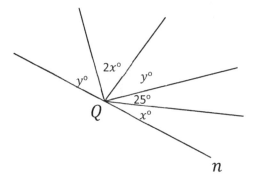

23. A container holds 3.5 gallons of water when it is $\frac{7}{24}$ full. How many gallons of water does the container hold when it's full?
    (A) 8
    (B) 12
    (C) 16
    (D) 20
    (E) 30

24. At a Zoo, the ratio of lions to tigers is 5 to 3. Which of the following could NOT be the total number of lions and tigers in the zoo?
    (A) 64
    (B) 80
    (C) 98
    (D) 104
    (E) 160

25. If x is greater than 48, then $\frac{1}{6}$ of x must be...
    (A) Greater than 12
    (B) Greater than 16
    (C) Equal to 16
    (D) Equal to 12
    (E) Less than 12

IF YOU FINISH BEFORE TIME IS CALLED, YOU MAY CHECK YOUR WORK ON THIS SECTION ONLY. DO NOT TURN TO ANY OTHER SECTION IN THE TEST. | STOP

SSAT Middle Level Math Practice Test 5

2019 - 2020

Two Parts

Total number of questions: 50

Section 1: 25 questions

Section 2: 25 questions

Total time for two parts: 60 Minutes

SSAT Practice Test 5 Answer Sheet

Remove (or photocopy) this answer sheet and use it to complete the practice test.

SSAT Middle Level Mathematics Practice Test 5 Answer Sheet

SSAT Middle Level Practice Test 5 Section 1

1	Ⓐ Ⓑ Ⓒ Ⓓ Ⓔ	11	Ⓐ Ⓑ Ⓒ Ⓓ Ⓔ	21	Ⓐ Ⓑ Ⓒ Ⓓ Ⓔ
2	Ⓐ Ⓑ Ⓒ Ⓓ Ⓔ	12	Ⓐ Ⓑ Ⓒ Ⓓ Ⓔ	22	Ⓐ Ⓑ Ⓒ Ⓓ Ⓔ
3	Ⓐ Ⓑ Ⓒ Ⓓ Ⓔ	13	Ⓐ Ⓑ Ⓒ Ⓓ Ⓔ	23	Ⓐ Ⓑ Ⓒ Ⓓ Ⓔ
4	Ⓐ Ⓑ Ⓒ Ⓓ Ⓔ	14	Ⓐ Ⓑ Ⓒ Ⓓ Ⓔ	24	Ⓐ Ⓑ Ⓒ Ⓓ Ⓔ
5	Ⓐ Ⓑ Ⓒ Ⓓ Ⓔ	15	Ⓐ Ⓑ Ⓒ Ⓓ Ⓔ	25	Ⓐ Ⓑ Ⓒ Ⓓ Ⓔ
6	Ⓐ Ⓑ Ⓒ Ⓓ Ⓔ	16	Ⓐ Ⓑ Ⓒ Ⓓ Ⓔ		
7	Ⓐ Ⓑ Ⓒ Ⓓ Ⓔ	17	Ⓐ Ⓑ Ⓒ Ⓓ Ⓔ		
8	Ⓐ Ⓑ Ⓒ Ⓓ Ⓔ	18	Ⓐ Ⓑ Ⓒ Ⓓ Ⓔ		
9	Ⓐ Ⓑ Ⓒ Ⓓ Ⓔ	19	Ⓐ Ⓑ Ⓒ Ⓓ Ⓔ		
10	Ⓐ Ⓑ Ⓒ Ⓓ Ⓔ	20	Ⓐ Ⓑ Ⓒ Ⓓ Ⓔ		

SSAT Middle Level Practice Test 5 Section 2

1	Ⓐ Ⓑ Ⓒ Ⓓ Ⓔ	11	Ⓐ Ⓑ Ⓒ Ⓓ Ⓔ	21	Ⓐ Ⓑ Ⓒ Ⓓ Ⓔ
2	Ⓐ Ⓑ Ⓒ Ⓓ Ⓔ	12	Ⓐ Ⓑ Ⓒ Ⓓ Ⓔ	22	Ⓐ Ⓑ Ⓒ Ⓓ Ⓔ
3	Ⓐ Ⓑ Ⓒ Ⓓ Ⓔ	13	Ⓐ Ⓑ Ⓒ Ⓓ Ⓔ	23	Ⓐ Ⓑ Ⓒ Ⓓ Ⓔ
4	Ⓐ Ⓑ Ⓒ Ⓓ Ⓔ	14	Ⓐ Ⓑ Ⓒ Ⓓ Ⓔ	24	Ⓐ Ⓑ Ⓒ Ⓓ Ⓔ
5	Ⓐ Ⓑ Ⓒ Ⓓ Ⓔ	15	Ⓐ Ⓑ Ⓒ Ⓓ Ⓔ	25	Ⓐ Ⓑ Ⓒ Ⓓ Ⓔ
6	Ⓐ Ⓑ Ⓒ Ⓓ Ⓔ	16	Ⓐ Ⓑ Ⓒ Ⓓ Ⓔ		
7	Ⓐ Ⓑ Ⓒ Ⓓ Ⓔ	17	Ⓐ Ⓑ Ⓒ Ⓓ Ⓔ		
8	Ⓐ Ⓑ Ⓒ Ⓓ Ⓔ	18	Ⓐ Ⓑ Ⓒ Ⓓ Ⓔ		
9	Ⓐ Ⓑ Ⓒ Ⓓ Ⓔ	19	Ⓐ Ⓑ Ⓒ Ⓓ Ⓔ		
10	Ⓐ Ⓑ Ⓒ Ⓓ Ⓔ	20	Ⓐ Ⓑ Ⓒ Ⓓ Ⓔ		

SSAT Middle Level Math

Practice Test 5

Section 1

25 questions

Total time for this test: 30 Minutes

You may NOT use a calculator on this part.

1. How long does a 420–miles trip take moving at 50 miles per hour (mph)?
   (A) 4 *hours*
   (B) 6 *hours and* 24 *minutes*
   (C) 8 *hours and* 24 *minutes*
   (D) 8 *hours and* 30 *minutes*
   (E) 10 *hours and* 30 *minutes*

2. The marked price of a computer is D dollar. Its price decreased by 20% in January and later increased by 10% in February. What is the final price of the computer in D dollar?
   (A) 0.80 D
   (B) 0.88 D
   (C) 0.90 D
   (D) 1.20 D
   (E) 1.40 D

3. If 0.55 equals $55M$, what is the value of M?
   (A) 0.01
   (B) 0.1
   (C) 1.0
   (D) 1.01
   (E) 1.001

4. Jason borrowed $4,800 for three months at an annual rate of 5%. How much interest did Jason owe?
   (A) $45
   (B) $60
   (C) $120
   (D) $240
   (E) $480

5. If three times a certain number, increased by 12, is equal to 39, what is the number?
   (A) 9
   (B) 12
   (C) 18
   (D) 27
   (E) 54

6. If 30 percent of a number is 150, then 12 percent of the same number is
   (A) 60
   (B) 72
   (C) 80
   (D) 90
   (E) 120

7. The average of $13, 15, 20$ and x is 18. What is the value of x?
    (A) 9
    (B) 15
    (C) 18
    (D) 20
    (E) 24

8. In five successive hours, a car traveled $40\ km, 45\ km, 50\ km, 35\ km$ and $55\ km$. In the next five hours, it traveled with an average speed of $50\ km\ per\ hour$. Find the total distance the car traveled in 10 hours.
    (A) $425\ km$
    (B) $450\ km$
    (C) $475\ km$
    (D) $500\ km$
    (E) $1,000\ km$

9. John has N toy cars. Jack has 4 more cars than John. If Jack gives John 3 cars, how many cars will Jack have, in terms of N?
    (A) N
    (B) $N - 1$
    (C) $N + 1$
    (D) $N + 2$
    (E) $N + 3$

10. What is the value of x in the following equation?

$$\frac{x + 4}{5} = 2$$

    (A) 2
    (B) 4
    (C) 6
    (D) 8
    (E) 10

11. The ratio of boys to girls in a school is $2:3$. If there are 600 students in a school, how many boys are in the school.
    (A) 540
    (B) 360
    (C) 300
    (D) 280
    (E) 240

12. Two third of 18 is equal to $\frac{2}{5}$ of what number?
   (A) 12
   (B) 20
   (C) 30
   (D) 60
   (E) 90

13. What is the cost of six ounces of cheese at $0.96 *per pound*?
   (A) $0.36
   (B) $0.40
   (C) $0.48
   (D) $0.52
   (E) $0.64

14. If 60% of A is 20% of B, then B is what percent of A?
   (A) 3%
   (B) 30%
   (C) 200%
   (D) 300%
   (E) 900%

15. Sophia purchased a sofa for $510. The sofa is regularly priced at $600. What was the percent discount Sophia received on the sofa?
   (A) 12%
   (B) 15%
   (C) 20%
   (D) 25%
   (E) 40%

16. A bag contains 18 balls: two green, five black, eight blue, a brown, a red and one white. If 17 balls are removed from the bag at random, what is the probability that a brown ball has been removed?
   (A) $\frac{1}{9}$
   (B) $\frac{1}{6}$
   (C) $\frac{16}{17}$
   (D) $\frac{17}{18}$
   (E) $\frac{1}{2}$

17. When a number is subtracted from 24 and the difference is divided by that number, the result is 3. What is the value of the number?
  (A) 2
  (B) 4
  (C) 6
  (D) 12
  (E) 24

18. If 40% of a class are girls, and 25% of girls play tennis, what percent of the class play tennis?
  (A) 10%
  (B) 15%
  (C) 20%
  (D) 40%
  (E) 80%

19. 55 students took an exam and 11 of them failed. What percent of the students passed the exam?
  (A) 20%
  (B) 40%
  (C) 60%
  (D) 80%
  (E) 90%

20. What is the value of x in the following equation?
$$3x + 10 = 49$$
  (A) 5
  (B) 7
  (C) 9
  (D) 11
  (E) 13

21. If $N \times \frac{4}{3} \times 5 = 0$, then $N = ...$
  (A) 0
  (B) 1
  (C) 2
  (D) 3
  (E) 4

22. Jason left a $12.00 tip on a lunch that cost $48.00, approximately what percentage was the tip?

    (A) 2.5%
    (B) 10%
    (C) 15%
    (D) 20%
    (E) 25%

23. If 40% of a number is 8, what is the number?

    (A) 4
    (B) 8
    (C) 10
    (D) 12
    (E) 20

24. If $\frac{z}{5} = 5$, then $z + 3 =$?

    (A) 4
    (B) 5
    (C) 15
    (D) 20
    (E) 28

25. In 1999, the average worker's income increased $2,000 per year starting from $28,000 annual salary. Which equation represents income greater than average? (I = income, x = number of years after 1999)

    (A) $I > 2,000x + 28,000$
    (B) $I > -2,000x + 28,000$
    (C) $I < -2,000x + 28,000$
    (D) $I < 2,000x - 28,000$
    (E) $I < 28,000x + 28,000$

IF YOU FINISH BEFORE TIME IS CALLED, YOU MAY CHECK YOUR WORK ON THIS SECTION ONLY. DO NOT TURN TO ANY OTHER SECTION IN THE TEST. **STOP**

SSAT Middle Level Math

Practice Test 5

Section 2

25 questions

Total time for this test: 30 Minutes

You may NOT use a calculator on this part.

1. Jacob has x dollars and he receives $150. He then buys a bicycle that costs $120. How much money does Jacob have now?
   (A) $x + 150$
   (B) $x + 120$
   (C) $x + 30$
   (D) $x - 120$
   (E) $x - 30$

2. What is the value of x in this equation?
$$\frac{x - 3}{8} + 4 = 20$$
   (A) 131
   (B) 128
   (C) 124
   (D) 120
   (E) 115

3. Ethan needs an 75% average in his writing class to pass. On his first 4 exams, he earned scores of 68%, 72%, 85%, and 90%. What is the minimum score Ethan can earn on his fifth and final test to pass?
   (A) 80%
   (B) 70%
   (C) 68%
   (D) 64%
   (E) 60%

4. The width of a rectangle is $6x$, the length is $8x$, and the perimeter is 56. What is the value of x?
   (A) 1
   (B) 2
   (C) 3
   (D) 4
   (E) 5

5. A bank is offering 4.5% simple interest on a savings account. If you deposit $8,000, how much interest will you earn in five years?
   (A) $360
   (B) $720
   (C) $1,800
   (D) $3,600
   (E) $4,800

6. If $(9 - 5) \times 4 = 8 + \square$, then $\square =?$
   (A) 5
   (B) 6
   (C) 7
   (D) 8
   (E) 9

7. Jason is 9 miles ahead of Joe running at 5.5 miles per hour and Joe is running at the speed of 7 miles per hour. How long does it take Joe to catch Jason?
   (A) $3 \ hours$
   (B) $4 \ hours$
   (C) $6 \ hours$
   (D) $8 \ hours$
   (E) $10 \ hours$

8. In a classroom, there are y tables that can each seat 5 people and there are x tables that can each seat 8 people. What is the number of people that can be seated in the classroom?
   (A) $5y$
   (B) $8x$
   (C) $8x - 5y$
   (D) 13
   (E) $8x + 5y$

9. The area of a circle is 64π. What is the diameter of the circle?
   (A) 4
   (B) 8
   (C) 12
   (D) 14
   (E) 16

10. A shirt costing $400 is discounted 15%. After a month, the shirt is discounted another 15%. Which of the following expressions can be used to find the selling price of the shirt?
    (A) $(400)\,(0.70)$
    (B) $(400) - 400\,(0.30)$
    (C) $(400)(0.15) - (400)\,(0.15)$
    (D) $(400)\,(0.85)\,(0.85)$
    (E) $(400)(0.85)(0.85) - (400)\,(0.15)$

11. Four one – foot rulers can be split among how many users to leave each with $\frac{1}{6}$ of a ruler?
    (A) 4
    (B) 6
    (C) 12
    (D) 24
    (E) 48

12. The perimeter of a rectangular yard is 60 meters. What is its length if its width is twice its length?
    (A) 10 *meters*
    (B) 18 *meters*
    (C) 20 *meters*
    (D) 24 *meters*
    (E) 36 *meters*

13. What is the value of x in this equation? $3x + 12 = 48$
    (A) 18
    (B) 14
    (C) 12
    (D) 10
    (E) 6

14. The mean of 50 test scores was calculated as 88. But, it turned out that one of the scores was misread as 94 but it was 69. What is the mean?
    (A) 85
    (B) 87
    (C) 87.5
    (D) 88.5
    (E) 90.5

15. The average of 6 numbers is 12. The average of 4 of those numbers is 10. What is the average of the other two numbers?
    (A) 10
    (B) 12
    (C) 14
    (D) 16
    (E) 24

16. If $x + 5 = 8, 2y - 1 = 5$ then $xy + 10 =$
    (A) 10
    (B) 19
    (C) 21
    (D) 27
    (E) 32

17. A card is drawn at random from a standard 52–card deck, what is the probability that the card is of Hearts? (The deck includes 13 of each suit clubs, diamonds, hearts, and spades)

    (A) $\frac{1}{3}$

    (B) $\frac{1}{4}$

    (C) $\frac{1}{6}$

    (D) $\frac{1}{52}$

    (E) $\frac{1}{104}$

18. Which of the following is NOT less than $\frac{1}{5}$?

    (A) $\frac{1}{8}$

    (B) $\frac{1}{2}$

    (C) $\frac{1}{9}$

    (D) $\frac{1}{10}$

    (E) $\frac{1}{7}$

19. Mr. Jones saves \$2,500 out of his monthly family income of \$55,000. What fractional part of his income does he save?

    (A) $\frac{1}{22}$

    (B) $\frac{1}{11}$

    (C) $\frac{3}{25}$

    (D) $\frac{2}{15}$

    (E) $\frac{1}{15}$

20. If $3x - 4 = 23$, then $2x + 6 =$?

    (A) 18

    (B) 20

    (C) 22

    (D) 24

    (E) 26

21. In two successive years, the population of a town is increased by 15% and 20%. What percent of the population is increased after two years?

    (A) 32%

    (B) 35%

    (C) 38%

    (D) 68%

    (E) 70%

22. If 150% of a number is 75, then what is the 90% of that number?
    (A) 45
    (B) 50
    (C) 70
    (D) 85
    (E) 90

23. What is the equivalent temperature of $104°F$ in Celsius? ($C = Celsius$)
$$C = \frac{5}{9}(F - 32)$$
    (A) 32
    (B) 40
    (C) 48
    (D) 52
    (E) 64

24. The perimeter of the trapezoid below is $36\ cm$. What is its area?

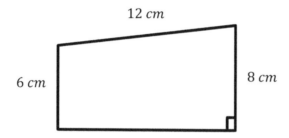

    (A) $48\ cm^2$
    (B) $70\ cm^2$
    (C) $140\ cm^2$
    (D) $576 cm^2$
    (E) $986 cm^2$

25. The width of a box is one third of its length. The height of the box is one third of its width. If the length of the box is $27\ cm$, what is the volume of the box?
    (A) $81\ cm^3$
    (B) $162\ cm^3$
    (C) $243\ cm^3$
    (D) $729\ cm^3$
    (E) $1880\ cm^3$

IF YOU FINISH BEFORE TIME IS CALLED, YOU MAY CHECK YOUR WORK ON THIS SECTION ONLY. DO NOT TURN TO ANY OTHER SECTION IN THE TEST.

STOP

SSAT Middle Level Math Practice Test Answers and Explanations

Now, it's time to review your results to see where you went wrong and what areas you need to improve

SSAT Middle Level Math Practice Test 1								SSAT Middle Level Math Practice Test 2							
Section 1				Section 2				Section 1				Section 2			
1	E	16	A	1	D	16	C	1	B	16	D	1	C	16	C
2	D	17	A	2	C	17	B	2	C	17	C	2	C	17	B
3	C	18	C	3	E	18	D	3	A	18	A	3	B	18	B
4	E	19	C	4	C	19	E	4	B	19	D	4	C	19	A
5	D	20	D	5	A	20	C	5	A	20	E	5	C	20	D
6	B	21	D	6	E	21	E	6	A	21	A	6	D	21	A
7	B	22	B	7	B	22	B	7	E	22	D	7	C	22	A
8	B	23	D	8	C	23	B	8	D	23	C	8	E	23	E
9	B	24	A	9	D	24	C	9	E	24	E	9	E	24	C
10	A	25	D	10	C	25	B	10	E	25	A	10	D	25	D
11	A			11	B			11	E			11	C		
12	C			12	E			12	C			12	A		
13	D			13	C			13	A			13	A		
14	C			14	D			14	C			14	A		
15	B			15	A			15	B			15	E		

SSAT Middle Level Math Practice Test 3								SSAT Middle Level Math Practice Test 4							
Section 1				**Section 2**				**Section 1**				**Section 2**			
1	B	16	E	1	E	16	A	1	D	16	B	1	C	16	C
2	C	17	C	2	E	17	B	2	D	17	A	2	C	17	B
3	B	18	C	3	C	18	A	3	B	18	C	3	C	18	C
4	A	19	E	4	B	19	C	4	A	19	C	4	D	19	D
5	B	20	D	5	B	20	C	5	E	20	D	5	A	20	C
6	C	21	A	6	E	21	E	6	A	21	D	6	D	21	E
7	E	22	E	7	C	22	E	7	B	22	B	7	B	22	B
8	C	23	A	8	E	23	A	8	B	23	D	8	C	23	B
9	D	24	C	9	C	24	C	9	B	24	D	9	D	24	C
10	E	25	E	10	D	25	C	10	D	25	A	10	C	25	A
11	C			11	C			11	A			11	B		
12	D			12	D			12	D			12	E		
13	B			13	D			13	D			13	D		
14	A			14	D			14	B			14	C		
15	A			15	D			15	E			15	C		

SSAT Middle Level Math Practice Test 5

	Section 1				Section 2		
1	C	16	D	1	C	16	B
2	B	17	C	2	A	17	B
3	A	18	A	3	E	18	B
4	B	19	D	4	B	19	A
5	A	20	E	5	C	20	D
6	A	21	A	6	D	21	C
7	E	22	E	7	C	22	A
8	C	23	E	8	E	23	B
9	C	24	E	9	E	24	B
10	C	25	A	10	D	25	D
11	E			11	D		
12	C			12	A		
13	A			13	C		
14	D			14	C		
15	B			15	D		

Score Your Test

SSAT scores are broken down by its three sections: Verbal, Mathematics, and Reading. A sum of the three sections is also reported.

For the Middle Level SSAT, the score range is 500-800, the lowest possible score a student can earn is 500 and the highest score is 800 for each section. A student receives 1 point for every correct answer and loses $\frac{1}{4}$ point for each incorrect answer. No points are lost by skipping a question.

The total scaled score for a Middle Level SSAT test is the sum of the scores for the Mathematics, verbal, and reading sections. A student will also receive a percentile score of between 1-99% that compares that student's test scores with those of other test takers of same grade and gender from the past 3 years.

Use the following table to convert SSAT Middle level raw score to scaled score.

SSAT Middle Level Math Scaled Scores	
Raw Scores	Mathematics
50	710
45	680
40	660
35	635
30	615
25	590
20	570
15	540
10	525
5	500
0	480
-5	460
- 10 and lower	440

SSAT Middle Level Mathematics Practice Test 1 Section 1

1) Choice E is correct

If 30 percent of a number is 60, then the number is: $30\% \ of \ x = 60 \rightarrow 0.3x = 60 \rightarrow x = \frac{60}{0.3} = \frac{600}{3} = 200$, 20 percent of 200 is: $20\% \ of \ 200 = \frac{20}{100} \times 200 = 40$

2) Choice D is correct

$2 \times 0.4 = 0.8$, all choices provided are equal to 0.8 except option D. $\frac{5}{15} \times 3 = 1$

3) Choice C is correct

Sara has M books. Mary has 6 more books than Sara. Then, Mary has $M + 6$ books. If Mary gives Sara 4 books, Mary will have: $M + 6 - 4 = M + 2$

4) Choice E is correct

If $\frac{x}{2} = 30$, then $\frac{3x}{2}$ is 3 times $\frac{x}{2}$. The answer is 90.

5) Choice D is correct

$\frac{1}{6}$ of 40 is 6.66. Let's review the choices provided:

(A) $0.3 \times 6 = 1.8$
(B) $0.3 \times 5 = 1.5$
(C) $0.2 \times 30 = 6$
(D) $0.2 \times 35 = 7$
(E) $0.2 \times 39.5 = 7.9$

Option D is the closest to 6.66

6) Choice B is correct

The diagonal of the square is 8. Let x be the side.

Use Pythagorean Theorem: $a^2 + b^2 = c^2$

$x^2 + x^2 = 8^2 \Rightarrow 2x^2 = 8^2 \Rightarrow 2x^2 = 64 \Rightarrow x^2 = 32 \Rightarrow x = \sqrt{32}$

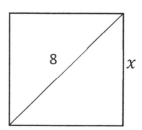

The area of the square is: $\sqrt{32} \times \sqrt{32} = 32$

7) Choice B is correct

The sum of supplement angles is 180. Let x be that angle. Therefore, $x + 5x = 180$

$6x = 180$, divide both sides by 6: $x = 30$

8) Choice B is correct

Use the formula for Percent of Change: $\dfrac{New\ Value - Old\ Value}{Old\ Value} \times 100\%$

$\dfrac{28-44}{44} \times 100\% \approx -36\%$ (negative sign here means that the new price is less than old price)

9) Choice B is correct

$One\ liter = 1,000\ cm^3 \rightarrow 6\ liters = 6,000 cm^3$, $6,000 = 25 \times 5 \times h \rightarrow h = \dfrac{6,000}{125} = 48\ cm$

10) Choice A is correct

The perimeter of the trapezoid is 64.

Therefore, the missing side (height) is $= 64 - 18 - 12 - 14 = 20$

Area of the trapezoid: $A = \dfrac{1}{2} h (b_1 + b_2) = \dfrac{1}{2} (10) (12 + 14) = 260$

11) Choice A is correct

If the score of Mia was 40, therefore the score of Ava is 20. Since, the score of Emma was half as that of Ava, therefore, the score of Emma is 10.

12) Choice C is correct

Let x be the number. Write the equation and solve for x. $\dfrac{2}{3} \times 9 = \dfrac{2}{5}$. $x \Rightarrow \dfrac{2 \times 9}{3} = \dfrac{2x}{5}$, use cross multiplication to solve for x. $5 \times 18 = 2x \times 3 \Rightarrow 90 = 6x \Rightarrow x = 15$

13) Choice D is correct

Let x be the number. Then: $3x + 5 = 32$ Solve for x: $3x + 5 = 32 \rightarrow 3x = 32 - 5 = 27 \rightarrow$

$$x = 27 \div 3 = 9$$

14) Choice C is correct

Simplify and solve for x in the equation. $4(x + 1) = 6(x - 4) + 20$, $4x + 4 = 6x - 24 + 20$, $4x + 4 = 6x - 4$. Subtract $4x$ from both sides: $4 = 2x - 4$, Add 4 to both sides: $8 = 2x$, $4 = x$

15) Choice B is correct

Let's write equations based on the information provided:

$Michelle = Karen - 9, Michelle = David - 4$, $Karen + Michelle + David = 82$

$Karen - 9 = Michelle \Rightarrow Karen = Michelle + 9$

$Karen + Michelle + David = 82$

Now, replace the ages of Karen and David by Michelle. Then:

$Michelle + 9 +\ Michelle + Michelle + 4\ = 82$

$3 \times Michelle + 13 = 82 \Rightarrow\ 3 \times Michelle\ =\ 82 - 13$

$3 \times Michelle = 69\ ,\ Michelle = 23$

16) Choice A is correct

Let x be one-kilogram orange cost, then:$2x + (2 \times 4.2) = 26.4 \rightarrow 2x + 8.4 = 26.4 \rightarrow$

$$2x = 26.4 - 8.4 \rightarrow 2x = 18 \rightarrow x = \frac{18}{2} = \$9$$

17) Choice A is correct

$average = \dfrac{sum\ of\ terms}{number\ of\ terms}$, The sum of the weight of all girls is: $18 \times 50 = 900kg$, The sum of the weight of all boys is: $32 \times 62 = 1,984\ kg$, The sum of the weight of all students is:

$900 +\ 1,984 = 2,884\ kg,\ Average = \frac{2,884}{50} = 57.68$

18) Choice C is correct

Solve for x in the equation. $6(x + 4) = 78 \rightarrow 6x + 24 = 78 \rightarrow 6x = 78 - 24 = 54 \rightarrow$

$$x = 54 \div 6 = 9$$

19) Choice C is correct

Let x be the number. Write the equation and solve for x. $(32 - x) \div\ x\ =\ 3$
Multiply both sides by x. $(32 - x) =\ 3x$, then add x both sides. $32 = 4x$, now divide both sides by 4. $x = 8$

20) Choice D is correct

Only option D is correct. $\frac{5}{6} = 0.83 \rightarrow 0.8 < \frac{5}{6}$

21) Choice D is correct

In a group of 5 books, the average number of pages is 24. Therefore, the sum of pages in all 5 books is $(5 \times 24 = 120)$. Mary adds a book with 36 pages to the group. Then, the sum of pages in all 6 books is $(5 \times 24 + 36 = 156)$. The new average number of pages per book is:$\frac{156}{6} = 26$

22) Choice B is correct

Choices A, C, D, and E are incorrect because 70% of each of the numbers is a non-whole number.

A. 49, $70\%\ of\ 49\ =\ 0.70 \times 49 = 34.3$
B. 40, $70\%\ of\ 40 = 0.70 \times 40 = 28$
C. 32, $70\%\ of\ 32 = 0.80 \times 32 = 22.4$

D. 12, $70\% \ of \ 12 = 0.70 \times 12 = 8.4$

E. 9, $70\% \ of \ 9 = 0.80 \times 9 = 6.3$

23) Choice D is correct

$$\frac{2}{5} \times 35 = \frac{70}{5} = 14$$

24) Choice A is correct

$$x = 25 + 125 = 150$$

25) Choice D is correct

The red box is 20% bigger than the blue box. Let x be the capacity of the blue box. Then:

$$x + 20\% \ of \ x = 36 \rightarrow 1.2x = 36 \rightarrow x = \frac{36}{1.2} = 30$$

SSAT Middle Level Mathematics Practice Test 1 Section 2

1) Choice D is correct

$\$8 \times 10 = \$80$, Petrol use: $10 \times 2 = 20$ liters, Petrol cost: $20 \times \$1 = \$20$

Money earned: $\$80 - \$20 = \$60$

2) Choice C is correct

From the choices provided, only C $\left(\frac{1}{7}\right)$ is less than $\frac{1}{5}$.

3) Choice E is correct

Amy earns $\$30.00 \ per \ hour$ now. $\$30.00 \ per \ hour$ is 20 percent more than her previous rate. Let x be her rate before her raise. Then: $x + 0.20x = 30 \rightarrow 1.2x = 30 \rightarrow x = \frac{30}{1.2} = 25$

John earns $\$28.80 \ per \ hour$ now. $\$28.80 \ per \ hour$ is 20 percent more than his previous rate. Let x be John's rate before his raise. Then: $x + 0.20x = 28.80 \rightarrow 1.2x = 28.80 \rightarrow x = \frac{28.80}{1.2} = 24$, Amy earned $\$1.00$ more per hour than John before their raises.

4) Choice C is correct.

Three people can paint 3 houses in 12 days. It means that for painting 6 houses in 12 days we need 6 people. To paint 6 houses in 6 days, 12 people are needed.

5) Choice A is correct.

$N \times (6 - 3) = 12 \rightarrow N \times 3 = 12 \rightarrow N = 4$

6) Choice E is correct.

The length of the rectangle is 24. Then, its width is 8. $24 \div 3 = 8$

$Perimeter \ of \ a \ rectangle = 2 \times width + 2 \times length = 2 \times 8 + 2 \times 24 = 16 + 48 = 64$

7) Choice B is correct

Let write angles A and B in the figure. $A = 180° - 112° = 68°$, $B = 180° - 145° = 40°$

The sum of all angles in a triangle is 180 degrees. Then: $x + A + B = 180° \rightarrow$

$$x = 180° - 68° - 40° = 72°$$

8) Choice C is correct.

If $x \blacksquare y = 4x + y - 2$, Then: $4 \blacksquare 12 = 4(4) + 12 - 2 = 16 + 12 - 2 = 26$

9) Choice D is correct

The width of a rectangle is $4x$ and its length is $6x$. Therefore, the perimeter of the rectangle is $20x$. $Perimeter\ of\ a\ rectangle = 2(width + length) = 2(4x + 6x) = 2(10x) = 20x$

The perimeter of the rectangle is 90. Then: $20x = 90 \rightarrow x = 4.5$

10) Choice C is correct

The area of the floor is: $7\ cm \times 24\ cm = 168\ cm^2$, The number is tiles needed $= 168 \div 8 = 21$

11) Choice B is correct

0.65 equals $65M$. Then: $65M = 0.65 \rightarrow M = \frac{0.65}{65} = 0.01$

12) Choice E is correct

$z = 3x + 5$, then, $2z = 2(3x + 5) = 6x + 10$, $2z + 3 = 6x + 10 + 3 = 6x + 13$

13) Choice C is correct.

$96 = 8x \times 4 \rightarrow x = 96 \div 4 = 24 \rightarrow x = 3$

x equals to 3. Let's review the choices provided:
A) $x + 4 \rightarrow 3 + 4 = 7$ 96 is not divisible by 9.
B) $2x - 4 \rightarrow 2 \times 3 - 1 = 5$ 96 is not divisible by 5.
C) $5x - 3 \rightarrow 5 \times 3 - 3 = 12$ 96 is divisible by 12.
D) $x \times 3 \rightarrow 3 \times 3 = 9$ 96 is not divisible by 9.
E) $3x + 1 \rightarrow 3 \times 3 + 1 = 10$ 96 is not divisible by 10.

The answer is C.

14) Choice D is correct

$\frac{1}{16} = 0.0625 \rightarrow C = 5, \frac{1}{25} = 0.04 \rightarrow D = 4 \rightarrow C \times D = 5 \times 4 = 20$

15) Choice A is correct

Use cross product to solve for x.

$$\frac{x}{x-2} = \frac{4}{5} \rightarrow 5 \times x = 4 \times (x - 2) \rightarrow 5x = 4x - 8 \rightarrow x = -8, x - 5 = -8 - 5 = -13$$

16) Choice C is correct

x is the number of all sales profit and 3% of it is: $3\% \times x = 0.03x$, Employer's revenue:

$$0.03x + 7,000$$

17) Choice B is correct

Number of biology book: 35, Total number of books; $35 + 85 + 90 = 210$

The ratio of the number of biology books to the total number of books is: $\frac{35}{210} = \frac{1}{6}$

18) Choice D is correct.

$5,000 + A - 200 = 7,400 \rightarrow 5,000 + A = 7,400 + 200 = 7,600 \rightarrow A = 7,600 - 5,000 = 2,600$

19) Choice E is correct

Let x be all expenses, then $\frac{22}{100}x = \$770 \rightarrow x = \frac{100 \times \$770}{22} = \$3,500$,

He spent for his rent: $\frac{27}{100} \times \$3,500 = \$945$

20) Choice C is correct

$5 \times M + 3 = 5 \rightarrow 5 \times M = 5 - 3 = 2 \rightarrow M = \frac{2}{5}$

21) Choice E is correct

$$\frac{52.6}{100} = 0.526$$

22) Choice B is correct

The angles on a straight line add up to 180 degrees. Then: $x + 22 + y + 2x + y = 180$, Then, $3x + 2y = 180 - 22 \rightarrow 3(28) + 2y = 158 \rightarrow 2y = 158 - 84 = 74 \rightarrow y = 37$

23) Choice B is correct

let x be the number of gallons of water the container holds when it is full.

Then; $\frac{5}{24}x = 2.5 \rightarrow x = \frac{24 \times 2.5}{5} = 12$

24) Choice C is correct.

The ratio of lions to tigers is 3 to 1 at the zoo. Therefore, total number of lions and tigers must be divisible by 4. From the choices provided, only 98 is not divisible by 4.

25) Choice B is correct

If x is greater than 18, then $\frac{1}{3}$ of x must be greater than: $\frac{1}{3} \times 18 = 6$.

SSAT Middle Level Mathematics Practice Test 2 Section 1

1) Choice B is correct

Use distance formula: $Distance = Rate \times time \Rightarrow 420 = 65 \times T$, divide both sides by 65. $420 \div 65 = T \Rightarrow T = 6.4 \ hours$. Change hours to minutes for the decimal part.

$$0.4 \ hours = 0.4 \times 60 = 24 \ minutes.$$

2) Choice C is correct

To find the discount, multiply the number by $(100\% - rate \ of \ discount)$.Therefore, for the first discount we get: $(D)(100\% - 15\%) = (D)(0.85) = 0.85 \ D$

For increase of 10%: $(0.85 \ D)(100\% + 10\%) = (0.85 \ D)(1.10) = 0.93 \ D = 93\% \ of \ D \ or \ 0.93D$

3) Choice A is correct

0.35 equals $350M$. Then: $0.35 = 350M \rightarrow M = \frac{0.35}{350} = 0.001$

4) Choice B is correct

Use simple interest formula: $I = prt$, (I = interest, p = principal, r = rate, t = time)

t is for one year. For 3 months, t is $\frac{1}{4}$ or 0.25. $I = (5,800)(0.05)(0.25) = 72.50$

5) Choice A is correct

Three times a certain number, increased by 10, is equal to 40. Write an equation and solve.

$$3x + 10 = 40 \rightarrow 3x = 40 - 10 = 30 \rightarrow x = \frac{30}{3} = 10$$

6) Choice A is correct

30 percent of a number is 150. Therefore, the number is 500. $0.30x = 150 \rightarrow x = \frac{150}{0.30} = 500$

15 percent of 500 is 75. $0.15 \times 500 = 75$

7) Choice E is correct

$$average = \frac{sum \ of \ terms}{number \ of \ terms} \Rightarrow 20 = \frac{13 + 15 + 20 + x}{4} \Rightarrow 80 = 48 + x \Rightarrow x = 32$$

8) Choice D is correct

Add the first 5 numbers. $40 + 45 + 50 + 35 + 55 = 225$

To find the distance traveled in the next 5 hours, multiply the average by number of hours.

$Distance = Average \times Rate = 55 \times 5 = 275$, Add both numbers. $275 + 225 = 500$

9) Choice E is correct

John has N toy cars. Jack has 6 more cars than John. Therefore, Jack has $N + 6$ toy cars. Jack gives John 3 cars. Now, Jack has $(N + 6 - 3)$ $N + 3$ toy cars.

10) Choice E is correct

$$\frac{x + 4}{5} = 3 \rightarrow x + 4 = 3 \times 5 = 15 \rightarrow x = 15 - 4 = 11$$

11) Choice E is correct

Th ratio of boy to girls is $2 : 3$. Therefore, there are 2 boys out of 5 students. To find the answer, first divide the total number of students by 5, then multiply the result by 2.

$$500 \div 5 = 100 \Rightarrow 100 \times 2 = 200$$

12) Choice C is correct

Let x be the number. Write the equation and solve for x. $\frac{2}{3} \times 24 = \frac{2}{5} . x \Rightarrow \frac{2 \times 24}{3} = \frac{2x}{5}$, use cross multiplication to solve for x. $5 \times 48 = 2x \times 3 \Rightarrow 240 = 6x \Rightarrow x = 40$

13) Choice A is correct

One pound of cheese costs $0.96. *One pound* $= 16$ *ounces*, 16 ounces of cheese costs $0.96. Then, 1 ounce of chees costs $(0.96 \div 16)$ $0.06. 7 ounces of cheese costs $(7 \times \$0.06)$ $0.42.

14) Choice C is correct

Write the equation and solve for B: $0.60A = 0.30B$, divide both sides by 0.30, then you will have $\frac{0.60}{0.30} A = B$, therefore: $B = 2A$, and B is 2 times of A or it's 200% of A.

15) Choice B is correct

$\frac{504}{600} = 0.84$. 504 is 84 percent of 600. So, the discount is 16%. $100\% - 16\% = 84\%$

16) Choice D is correct

If 17 balls are removed from the bag at random, there will be one ball in the bag. The probability of choosing a brown ball is 1 out of 18. Therefore, the probability of not choosing a brown ball is 17 out of 18 and the probability of having not a brown ball after removing 17 balls is the same.

17) Choice C is correct

Let x be the number. Write the equation and solve for x. $(28 - x) \div x = 3$. Multiply both sides by x. $(28 - x) = 3x$, then add x both sides. $28 = 4x$, now divide both sides by 4. $x = 7$

18) Choice A is correct

The percent of girls playing tennis is: $45\% \times 25\% = 0.45 \times 0.25 \approx 0.11 = 11\%$

19) Choice D is correct

The failing rate is 11 out of $44 = \frac{11}{55}$. Change the fraction to percent: $\frac{11}{44} \times 100\% = 25\%$

25 percent of students failed. Therefore, 75 percent of students passed the exam.

20) Choice E is correct

$3x + 10 = 67 \rightarrow 3x = 67 - 10 = 57 \rightarrow x = \dfrac{57}{3} = 19$

21) Choice A is correct

$N \times \frac{4}{3} \times 7 = 0$, then N must be 0.

22) Choice D is correct

$12 is what percent of $60? $12 \div 60 = 0.20 = 20\%$

23) Choice C is correct

Let x be the number. Write the equation and solve for x.

$60\% \; of \; x = 6 \Rightarrow 0.60 \, x = 6 \Rightarrow x = 6 \div 0.60 = 10$

24) Choice E is correct

$\frac{z}{5} = 4 \rightarrow z = 4 \times 5 = 20, z + 3 = 20 + 3 = 23$

25) Choice A is correct

Let x be the number of years. Therefore, $3,000 per year equals $3000x$. starting from $24,000 annual salary means you should add that amount to $2000x$. Income more than that is:

$I > 3000x + 24000$

SSAT Middle Level Mathematics Practice Test 2 Section 2

1) Choice C is correct

John has x dollars and he receives $150. Therefore, he has $x + 150$.

He then buys a bicycle that costs \$110. Now, he has: $x + 150 - 110 = x + 40$

2) Choice C is correct

$$\frac{x-3}{8} + 5 = 20 \rightarrow \frac{x-3}{8} = 20 - 5 = 15 \rightarrow x - 3 = 15 \times 8 = 120 \rightarrow$$
$$x = 120 + 3 = 123$$

3) Choice B is correct

Bob needs an 78% average to pass for five exams. Therefore, the sum of 5 exams must be at lease $5 \times 78 = 390$, The sum of 4 exams is: $68 + 72 + 85 + 90 = 315$.

The minimum score Bob can earn on his fifth and final test to pass is: $390 - 315 = 75$

4) Choice C is correct

The width of a rectangle is $6x$ and its length is $8x$. Then, the perimeter of the rectangle is $28x$.

Perimeter of a rectangle $= 2(width + length) = 2(6x + 8x) = 28x$

The perimeter of the rectangle is 84. Then: $28x = 84 \rightarrow x = 3$

5) Choice C is correct

Use simple interest formula: $I = prt$, ($I =$ interest, $p =$ principal, $r =$ rate, $t =$ time)

$I = (8,000)(0.035)(5) = 1,400$

6) Choice D is correct

$(8 - 4) \times 4 = 8 + \square$

Then: $4 \times 4 = 8 + \square$, $16 = 8 + \square$, then $\square = 8$

7) Choice C is correct

The distance between Jason and Joe is 9 miles. Jason running at 6.5 miles per hour and Joe is running at the speed of 8 miles per hour. Therefore, every hour the distance is 1.5 miles less.

$9 \div 1.5 = 6$

8) Choice E is correct

There are y tables that can each seat 4 people and there are x tables that can each seat 8 people. Therefore, $4y + 8x$ people can be seated in the classroom

9) Choice E is correct

The formula for the area of the circle is: $A = \pi r^2$

The area of the circle is 81π. Therefore: $A = \pi r^2 \Rightarrow 81\pi = \pi r^2$, Divide both sides by π: $81 = r^2 \Rightarrow r = 9$, Diameter of a circle is $2 \times$ radius. Then: Diameter $= 2 \times 9 = 18$

10) Choice D is correct

To find the discount, multiply the number by $(100\% - rate\ of\ discount)$. Therefore, for the first discount we get: $(300)\ (100\% - 15\%) = (300)\ (0.85)$, For the next 15% discount: $(300)\ (0.85)\ (0.85)$

11) Choice C is correct

$$4 \div \frac{1}{3} = 12$$

12) Choice A is correct

The width of the rectangle is twice its length. Let x be the length. Then, $width = 2x$

Perimeter of the rectangle is $2\ (width + length) = 2(2x + x) = 72 \Rightarrow 6x = 72 \Rightarrow x = 12$

Length of the rectangle is 12 meters.

13) Choice A is correct

$$2x + 10 = 48 \rightarrow 2x = 48 - 10 = 38 \rightarrow x = \frac{38}{2} = 19$$

14) Choice A is correct

$$average\ (mean) = \frac{sum\ of\ terms}{number\ of\ terms} \Rightarrow 86 = \frac{sum\ of\ terms}{50} \Rightarrow sum = 86 \times 50 = 4300$$

The difference of 94 and 69 is 25. Therefore, 25 should be subtracted from the sum.

$$4300 - 25 = 4275,\ mean = \frac{sum\ of\ terms}{number\ of\ terms} \Rightarrow mean = \frac{4275}{50} = 85.5$$

15) Choice E is correct

$$average = \frac{sum\ of\ terms}{number\ of\ terms} \Rightarrow (average\ of\ 6\ numbers)\ 15 = \frac{sum\ of\ numbers}{6} \Rightarrow sum\ of\ 6\ numbers$$
is $15 \times 6 = 90$

$(average\ of\ 4\ numbers)\ 10 = \frac{sum\ of\ numbers}{4} \Rightarrow$ sum of 4 numbers is $10 \times 4 = 40$

$sum\ of\ 6\ numbers - sum\ of\ 4\ numbers = sum\ of\ 2\ numbers$

$90 - 40 = 50$ average of 2 numbers $= \frac{50}{2} = 25$

16) Choice C is correct

$x + 5 = 8 \rightarrow x = 8 - 5 = 3, 2y - 1 = 5 \rightarrow 2y = 6 \rightarrow y = 3, xy + 15 = 3 \times 3 + 15 = 24$

17) Choice B is correct

The probability of choosing a Hearts is $\frac{13}{52} = \frac{1}{4}$

18) Choice B is correct

From the choices provided, only $\frac{1}{3}$ is greater than $\frac{1}{5}$.

19) Choice A is correct

2,500 out of 65,000 equals to $\frac{2500}{65000} = \frac{25}{650} = \frac{1}{26}$

20) Choice D is correct

$5x - 6 = 39 \to 5x = 39 + 6 = 45 \to x = 9$, then $3x + 6 = 3 \times 9 + 6 = 27 + 6 = 33$

21) Choice A is correct

the population is increased by 10% and 20%. 10% increase changes the population to 110% of original population. For the second increase, multiply the result by 120%.

$(1.10) \times (1.20) = 1.32 = 132\%$, 32 percent of the population is increased after two years.

22) Choice A is correct

First, find the number. Let x be the number. Write the equation and solve for x.

150% of a number is 75, then: $1.5 \times x = 75 \Rightarrow x = 75 \div 1.5 = 50$. 80% of 50 is: $0.8 \times 50 = 40$

23) Choice E is correct

Plug in 104 for F and then solve for C.

$$C = \frac{5}{9}(F - 32) \Rightarrow C = \frac{5}{9}(140 - 32) \Rightarrow C = \frac{5}{9}(108) = 60$$

24) Choice C is correct

The perimeter of the trapezoid is 50.

Therefore, the missing side (height) is $= 50 - 8 - 12 - 6 = 24$

Area of a trapezoid: $A = \frac{1}{2}h(b_1 + b_2) = \frac{1}{2}(24)(6 + 8) = 168$

25) Choice D is correct

If the length of the box is 24, then the width of the box is one third of it, 8, and the height of the box is 4 (half of the width). The volume of the box is:

$Volume \; of \; a \; box = (length) \times (width) \times (height) = (24) \times (8) \times (4) = 768$

SSAT Middle Level Mathematics Practice Test 3 Section 1

1) Choice B is correct

30 percent of a number is 180. Therefore, the number is 600.

$0.30x = 180 \rightarrow x = \frac{180}{0.30} = 600$, 12 percent of 600 is 72. $0.12 \times 600 = 72$

2) Choice C is correct

0.45 equals $4.5F$. $0.45 = 4.5F \rightarrow F = \frac{0.45}{4.5} = 0.1$. Then: $10F = 10 \times 0.1 = 1$

3) Choice B is correct

Use simple interest formula: $I = prt$ (I = interest, p = principal, r = rate, t = time)

t is for one year. For 3 months, t is $\frac{1}{4}$ or 0.25, $I = (5,800)(0.04)(0.25) = 58$

4) Choice A is correct

Three times a certain number, increased by 6, is equal to 30. Write an equation and solve.

$3x + 6 = 30 \rightarrow 3x = 30 - 6 = 24 \rightarrow x = \frac{24}{3} = 8$

5) Choice B is correct

Use distance formula: $Distance = Rate \times time \Rightarrow 320 = 50 \times T$,

divide both sides by 50. $320 \div 50 = T \Rightarrow T = 6.4\ hours$.

Change hours to minutes for the decimal part. $0.4\ hours = 0.4 \times 60 = 24\ minutes$.

6) Choice C is correct

To find the discount, multiply the number by $(100\% - rate\ of\ discount)$.

Therefore, for the first discount we get: $(D)(100\% - 15\%) = (D)(0.85) = 0.85\ D$

For increase of 15%: $(0.85\ D)(100\% + 15\%) = (0.85\ D)(1.15) = 0.97\ D = 97\%\ of\ D$

7) Choice E is correct

$average = \frac{sum\ of\ terms}{number\ of\ terms} \Rightarrow 20 = \frac{14+16+21+}{4} \Rightarrow 80 = 51 + x \Rightarrow x = 29$

8) Choice C is correct

$$\frac{x+4}{2} = 6 \rightarrow x + 4 = 2 \times 6 = 12 \rightarrow x = 12 - 4 = 8$$

9) Choice D is correct

John has M toy cars. Jack has 5 more cars than John. Therefore, Jack has $M + 5$ toy cars. Jack gives John 2 cars. Now, Jack has $(M + 5 - 2)$ $M + 3$ toy cars.

10) Choice E is correct

Write the equation and solve for B: $0.12A = 0.03B$, divide both sides by 0.03, then you will have $\frac{0.12}{0.03}A = B$, therefore: $B = 4A$, and B is 4 times of A or it's 400% of A.

11) Choice C is correct

The ratio of boy to girls is $3 : 2$. Therefore, there are 3 boys out of 5 students. To find the answer, first divide the total number of students by 5, then multiply the result by 3.

$$600 \div 5 = 120 \Rightarrow 120 \times 3 = 360$$

12) Choice D is correct

Add the first 5 numbers. $41 + 46 + 52 + 36 + 51 = 226$

To find the distance traveled in the next 5 hours, multiply the average by number of hours.

$Distance = Average \times Rate = 60 \times 5 = 300$, Add both numbers. $300 + 226 = 526$

13) Choice B is correct

Let x be the number. Write the equation and solve for x. $\frac{2}{3} \times 45 = \frac{4}{5} \times x \Rightarrow \frac{2 \times 45}{3} = \frac{4x}{5}$, use cross multiplication to solve for x. $5 \times 90 = 4x \times 3 \Rightarrow 450 = 12x \Rightarrow x = 37.5$

14) Choice A is correct

One pound of cheese costs 0.80. $One \ pound = 16 \ ounces$, 16 ounces of cheese costs 0.87. Then, 1 ounce of chees costs $(0.87 \div 16)$ 0.05. 6 ounces of cheese costs $(6 \times \$0.05)$ 0.30.

15) Choice A is correct

The percent of girls playing tennis is: $30\% \times 20\% = 0.30 \times 0.20 = 0.06 = 6\%$

16) Choice E is correct

$\frac{414}{600} = 0.69 = 69\%$. So, the discount is 31%.

17) Choice C is correct

Let x be the number. Write the equation and solve for x. $(36 - x) \div x = 3$, Multiply both sides by x. $(36 - x) = 3x$, then add x both sides. $36 = 4x$, now divide both sides by 4. $x = 9$

18) Choice C is correct

The failing rate is 12 out of $55 = \frac{12}{50}$, Change the fraction to percent: $\frac{12}{50} \times 100\% = 24\%$

24 percent of students failed. Therefore, 76 percent of students passed the exam.

19) Choice E is correct

$$3x + 10 = 46 \rightarrow 3x = 46 - 10 = 36 \rightarrow x = \frac{36}{3} = 12$$

20) Choice D is correct

If 18 balls are removed from the bag at random, there will be one ball in the bag. The probability of choosing a brown ball is 1 out of 19. Therefore, the probability of not choosing a brown ball is 18 out of 19 and the probability of having not a brown ball after removing 18 balls is the same.

21) Choice A is correct

$M \times \frac{4}{3} \times 4 = 1$, then $M \times \frac{16}{3} = 1$. Multiply both sides by $\frac{3}{16}$. $M \times \frac{16}{3} \times \frac{3}{16} = 1 \times \frac{3}{16} \rightarrow \frac{3 \times 16}{3 \times 16} M = \frac{3}{16} \rightarrow$ $M = \frac{3}{16}$

22) Choice E is correct

$4.50 is what percent of $30? $4.5 \div 30 = 0.15 = 15\%$

23) Choice A is correct

Let x be the number of years. Therefore, $3,000 per year equals $3000x$. starting from $25,000 annual salary means you should add that amount to $3000x$. Income more than that is:

$$I > 3,000x + 25,000$$

24) Choice C is correct

Let x be the number. Write the equation and solve for x. 50% of $x = 5 \Rightarrow 0.5x = 5 \Rightarrow$

$$x = 5 \div 0.50 = 10$$

25) Choice E is correct

$\frac{z}{5} = 4 \rightarrow z = 4 \times 5 = 20 , z + 5 = 20 + 5 = 25$

SSAT Middle Level Mathematics Practice Test 3 Section 2

1) Choice E is correct

$(10 - 5) \times 4 = 10 + \square$

Then: $5 \times 4 = 10 + \square$, $20 = 10 + \square$, then $\square = 10$

2) Choice E is correct

$\dfrac{x-3}{5} + 5 = 20 \rightarrow \dfrac{x-3}{5} = 20 - 5 = 15 \rightarrow x - 3 = 15 \times 5 = 75 \rightarrow$

$x = 75 + 3 = 78$

3) Choice C is correct

Use simple interest formula: $I = prt$ (I = interest, p = principal, r = rate, t = time)

$I = (7,000)(0.055)(5) = 1,925$

4) Choice B is correct

Emma needs an 75% average to pass for five exams. Therefore, the sum of 5 exams must be at least $5 \times 75 = 375$, the sum of 4 exams is: $68 + 75 + 80 + 90 = 313$.

The minimum score Emma can earn on her fifth and final test to pass is: $375 - 313 = 62$

5) Choice B is correct

The width of a rectangle is $4x$ and its length is $6x$. Then, the perimeter of the rectangle is $20x$.

$Perimeter\ of\ a\ rectangle = 2(width + length) = 2(4x + 6x) = 20x$

The perimeter of the rectangle is 40. Then: $20x = 40 \rightarrow x = 2$

6) Choice E is correct

There are y tables that can each seat 4 people and there are x tables that can each seat 7 people. Therefore, $4y + 7x$ people can be seated in the classroom.

7) Choice C is correct

John has x dollars and he receives \$150. Therefore, he has $x + 150$. He then buys a bicycle that costs \$130. Now, he has: $x + 150 - 130 = x + 20$

8) Choice E is correct

The distance between Jason and Joe is 15 miles. Jason running at 5.5 miles per hour and Joe is running at the speed of 7 miles per hour. Therefore, every hour the distance is 1.5 miles less. $15 \div 1.5 = 10$

9) Choice C is correct

$5 \div \dfrac{1}{5} = 25$

10) Choice D is correct

The formula for the area of the circle is: $= \pi r^2$, The area of the circle is 49π. Therefore:

$A = \pi r^2 \Rightarrow 49\pi = \pi r^2$, Divide both sides by π: $49 = r^2 \Rightarrow r = 7$

Diameter of a circle is $2 \times$ radius. Then: Diameter $= 2 \times 7 = 14$

11) Choice C is correct

The width of the rectangle is twice its length. Let x be the length. Then, $width = 2x$, Perimeter of the rectangle is $2 \, (width + length) = 2(2x + x) = 120 \Rightarrow 6x = 120 \Rightarrow x = 20$

Length of the rectangle is 20 meters.

12) Choice D is correct

To find the discount, multiply the number by $(100\% - rate\ of\ discount)$.

Therefore, for the first discount we get: $(300) \, (100\% - 20\%) = (300) \, (0.80)$

For the next 15% discount: $(300) \, (0.80) \, (0.85)$

13) Choice D is correct

$average = \frac{sum\ of\ terms}{number\ of\ terms} \Rightarrow$ (average of 6 numbers) $14 = \frac{sum\ of\ numbers}{6} \Rightarrow$ sum of 6 numbers is : $14 \times 6 = 84$.

(average of 4 numbers) $10 = \frac{sum\ of\ numbers}{4} \Rightarrow$ sum of 4 numbers is $10 \times 4 = 40$

$sum\ of\ 6\ numbers - sum\ of\ 4\ numbers = sum\ of\ 2\ numbers$

$84 - 40 = 44 \qquad$ average of 2 numbers $= \frac{44}{2} = 22$

14) Choice D is correct

$3x + 10 = 37 \rightarrow 3x = 37 - 10 = 27 \rightarrow x = \frac{27}{3} = 9$

15) Choice D is correct

$x + 4 = 8 \rightarrow x = 8 - 4 = 4$, $2y - 3 = 5 \rightarrow 2y = 8 \rightarrow y = 4$, $xy + 10 = 4 \times 4 + 10 = 26$

16) Choice A is correct

The deck contains 13 Spades. Then, the probability of choosing a Spades is $\frac{13}{52} = \frac{1}{4}$

17) Choice B is correct

From the choices provided, only $\frac{1}{4}$ is greater than $\frac{1}{5}$.

18) Choice A is correct

2,500 out of 75,000 equals to $\frac{2,500}{75,000} = \frac{25}{750} = \frac{1}{30}$

19) Choice C is correct

$$average\ (mean) = \frac{sum\ of\ terms}{number\ of\ terms} \Rightarrow 90 = \frac{sum\ of\ terms}{50} \Rightarrow sum = 90 \times 50 = 4,500$$

The difference of 84 and 59 is 25. Therefore, 25 should be subtracted from the sum.

$$4,500 - 25 = 4,475, mean = \frac{sum\ of\ terms}{number\ of\ terms} \Rightarrow mean = \frac{4,475}{50} = 89.5$$

20) Choice C is correct

$3x - 5 = 19 \Rightarrow 3x = 24 \Rightarrow x = 8$, then $2x + 6 = 2 \times 8 + 6 = 16 + 6 = 22$

21) Choice E is correct

Plug in 167 for F and then solve for C.

$$C = \frac{5}{9}(F - 32) \Rightarrow C = \frac{5}{9}(167 - 32) \Rightarrow C = \frac{5}{9}(135) = 75$$

22) Choice E is correct

If the length of the box is 36, then the width of the box is one third of it, 12, and the height of the box is 6(half of the width). The volume of the box is:

$$Volume\ of\ a\ box = (length) \times (width) \times (height) = (36) \times (12) \times (6) = 2,592$$

23) Choice A is correct

First, find the number. Let x be the number. Write the equation and solve for x. 150% of a number is 45, then: $1.5 \times x = 45 \Rightarrow x = 45 \div 1.5 = 30$, 80% of 30 is: $0.8 \times 30 = 24$

24) Choice C is correct

The perimeter of the trapezoid is 46. Therefore, the missing side (height) is =

$46 - 7 - 12 - 5 = 22$. Area of a trapezoid: $A = \frac{1}{2}h(b_1 + b_2) = \frac{1}{2}(22)(5 + 7) = 132$

25) Choice C is correct

the population is increased by 16% and 20%. 16% increase changes the population to 116% of original population. For the second increase, multiply the result by 120%.

$(1.16) \times (1.20) = 1.39 = 139\%$, 39 percent of the population is increased after two years.

SSAT Middle Level Mathematics Practice Test 4 Section 1

1) Choice D is correct

If 15 percent of a number is 60, then the number is: $15\% \ of \ x = 60 \to 0.15x = 60 \to x = \frac{60}{0.15} =$ 400, 25 percent of 400 is: $25\% \ of \ 200 = \frac{25}{100} \times 400 = 100$

2) Choice D is correct

$0.2 \times 4 = 0.8$, all choices provided are equal to 0.8 except choice D. $\frac{5}{15} \times 3 = 1$

3) Choice B is correct

Sara has N books. Mary has 5 more books than Sara. Then, Mary has $N + 5$ books. If Mary gives Sara 4 books, Mary will have: $N + 5 - 4 = N + 1$

4) Choice A is correct

If $\frac{3x}{2} = 30$, then $3x = 60 \to x = 20$, $\frac{2x}{5} = \frac{2 \times 20}{5} = \frac{40}{5} = 8$

5) Choice E is correct

$\frac{1}{5}$ of 40 is 8. Let's review the choices provided:

    (A) $0.3 \times 6 = 1.8$
    (B) $0.3 \times 5 = 1.5$
    (C) $0.2 \times 30 = 6$
    (D) $0.2 \times 35 = 7$
    (E) $0.2 \times 39.5 = 7.9$

Option E is the closest to 8.

6) Choice A is correct

The diagonal of the square is 6. Let x be the side.

Use Pythagorean Theorem: $a^2 + b^2 = c^2$

$x^2 + x^2 = 6^2 \Rightarrow 2x^2 = 6^2 \Rightarrow 2x^2 = 36 \Rightarrow x^2 = 18 \Rightarrow x = \sqrt{18}$

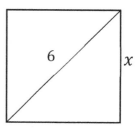

The area of the square is: $\sqrt{18} \times \sqrt{18} = 18$

7) Choice B is correct

The sum of supplement angles is 180. Let x be that angle. Therefore, $x + 8x = 180$

$9x = 180$, divide both sides by 9: $x = 20$

8) Choice B is correct

Use the formula for Percent of Change: $\dfrac{New\ Value - Old\ Value}{Old\ Value} \times 100\%$

$\dfrac{28-40}{40} \times 100\% = -30\%$ (negative sign here means that the new price is less than old price)

9) Choice B is correct

$x = 20 + 125 = 145$

10) Choice D is correct

The perimeter of the trapezoid is 54.

Therefore, the missing side (height) is $= 54 - 18 - 12 - 14 = 10$

Area of the trapezoid: $A = \frac{1}{2} h (b_1 + b_2) = \frac{1}{2} (10) (12 + 14) = 130$

11) Choice A is correct

If the score of Mia was 60, therefore the score of Ava is 30. Since, the score of Emma was half as that of Ava, therefore, the score of Emma is 15.

12) Choice D is correct

Let x be the number. Write the equation and solve for x.

$\frac{2}{3} \times 30 = \frac{2}{5} \times x \Rightarrow \frac{2 \times 30}{3} = \frac{2x}{5}$, use cross multiplication to solve for x.

$5 \times 60 = 2x \times 3 \Rightarrow 300 = 6x \Rightarrow x = 50$

13) Choice D is correct

Let x be the number. Then: $3x + 6 = 30$, Solve for x: $3x + 6 = 30 \rightarrow 3x = 30 - 6 = 24 \rightarrow x = 24 \div 3 = 8$

14) Choice B is correct

Simplify and solve for x in the equation. $4(x + 2) = 6(x - 4) + 20 \rightarrow 4x + 8 = 6x - 24 + 20$

$4x + 8 = 6x - 4$, Subtract $4x$ from both sides: $8 = 2x - 4$, Add 4 to both sides: $12 = 2x, 6 = x$

15) Choice E is correct

Five years ago, Amy was three times as old as Mike. Mike is 10 years now. Therefore, 5 years ago Mike was 5 years. Five years ago, Amy was: $A = 3 \times 5 = 15$

Now Amy is 20 years old: $15 + 5 = 20$

16) Choice B is correct

Let x be one-kilogram orange cost, then: $3x + (2 \times 4.2) = 26.4 \rightarrow 3x + 8.4 = 26.4 \rightarrow$ $3x = 26.4 - 8.4 \rightarrow 3x = 18 \rightarrow x = \frac{18}{3} = \$6$

17) Choice A is correct

$average = \frac{sum\ of\ terms}{number\ of\ terms}$, The sum of the weight of all girls is: $18 \times 60 = 1080\ kg$, The sum of the weight of all boys is: $32 \times 62 = 1984\ kg$, The sum of the weight of all students is: $1,080 + 1,984 = 3,064\ kg$, $Average = \frac{3064}{50} = 61.28$

18) Choice C is correct

Solve for x in the equation. $6(x + 4) = 72 \rightarrow 6x + 24 = 72 \rightarrow 6x = 72 - 24 = 48 \rightarrow x = 48 \div 6 = 8$

19) Choice C is correct

Let x be the number. Write the equation and solve for x. $(20 - x) \div x = 3$
Multiply both sides by x. $(20 - x) = 3x$, then add x both sides. $20 = 4x$, now divide both sides by 4. $x = 5$

20) Choice D is correct

Only option D is correct. $\frac{5}{6} = 0.83 \rightarrow 0.8 < \frac{5}{6}$

21) Choice D is correct

In a group of 5 books, the average number of pages is 24. Therefore, the sum of pages in all 5 books is $(5 \times 24 = 120)$. Mary adds a book with 30 pages to the group. Then, the sum of pages in all 6 books is $(5 \times 24 + 30 = 150)$. The new average number of pages per book is: $\frac{150}{6} = 25$

22) Choice B is correct

Choices A, C, D, and E are incorrect because 80% of each of the numbers is a non-whole number.

    A. 49 $80\%\ of\ 49 = 0.80 \times 49 = 39.2$
    B. 35 $80\%\ of\ 35 = 0.80 \times 35 = 28$
    C. 32 $80\%\ of\ 32 = 0.80 \times 32 = 25.6$
    D. 12 $80\%\ of\ 12 = 0.80 \times 12 = 9.6$
    E. 8 $80\%\ of\ 8 = 0.80 \times 8 = 6.4$

23) Choice D is correct

$\frac{2}{5} \times 25 = \frac{50}{5} = 10$

24) Choice D is correct

The red box is 20% greater than the blue box. Let x be the capacity of the blue box. Then:

$$x + 20\% \ of \ x = 30 \rightarrow 1.2x = 30 \rightarrow x = \frac{30}{1.2} = 25$$

25) Choice A is correct

One liter $= 1,000 \ cm^3 \rightarrow 6 \ liters = 6,000 \ cm^3$. Let's put h for the height of the water. Then:

$$6,000 = 15 \times 5 \times h \rightarrow h = \frac{6,000}{75} = 80 \ cm$$

SSAT Middle Level Mathematics Practice Test 4 Section 2

1) Choice C is correct

$\$9 \times 10 = \$90$, Petrol use: $10 \times 2 = 20$ liters, Petrol cost: $20 \times \$1 = \$20$

Money earned: $\$90 - \$20 = \$70$

2) Choice C is correct

From the choices provided, only C $\left(\frac{1}{6}\right)$ is less than $\frac{1}{5}$.

3) Choice C is correct

Amy earns $\$30.00 \ per \ hour$ now. $\$30.00 \ per \ hour$ is 20 percent more than her previous rate. Let x be her rate before her raise. Then: $x + 0.20x = 30 \rightarrow 1.2x = 30 \rightarrow x = \frac{30}{1.2} = 25$

John earns $\$26.40 \ per \ hour$ now. $\$26.40 \ per \ hour$ is 20 percent more than his previous rate. Let x be John's rate before his raise. Then: $x + 0.20x = 26.40 \rightarrow 1.2x = 26.40 \rightarrow x = \frac{26.40}{1.2} = 22$, Amy earned $\$3.00$ more per hour than John before their raises.

4) Choice D is correct.

Four people can paint 4 houses in 10 days. It means that for painting 8 houses in 10 days we need 8 people. To paint 8 houses in 5 days, 16 people are needed.

5) Choice A is correct.
$N \times (5 - 3) = 12 \rightarrow N \times 2 = 12 \rightarrow N = 6$

6) Choice D is correct.

The length of the rectangle is 18. Then, its width is 6. $18 \div 3 = 6$

   Perimeter of a rectangle $= 2 \times width + 2 \times length = 2 \times 6 + 2 \times 18 = 12 + 36 = 48$

7) Choice B is correct

$\alpha = 180° - 112° = 68°$, $b = 180° - 135° = 45°$, The sum of all angles in a triangle is 180 degrees. Then:$x + \alpha + b = 180° \rightarrow x = 180° - 68° - 45° = 67°$

8) Choice C is correct.

If $x \blacksquare y = 3x + y - 2$, Then: $4 \blacksquare 12 = 3(4) + 12 - 2 = 12 + 12 - 2 = 22$

9) Choice D is correct

The width of a rectangle is $4x$ and its length is $6x$. Therefore, the perimeter of the rectangle is $20x$. $Perimeter\ of\ a\ rectangle = 2(width + length) = 2(4x + 6x) = 2(10x) = 20x$

The perimeter of the rectangle is 80. Then: $20x = 80 \rightarrow x = 4$

10) Choice C is correct

The area of the floor is: $6\ cm \times 24\ cm = 144\ cm^2$, The number is tiles needed $= 144 \div 8 = 18$

11) Choice B is correct

0.45 equals $450M$. Then: $450M = 0.45 \rightarrow M = \frac{0.45}{450} = 0.001$

12) Choice E is correct

$z = 3x + 6$, then, $2z = 2(3x + 6) = 6x + 12$, $2z + 3 = 6x + 12 + 3 = 6x + 15$

13) Choice D is correct.

$20 = 2x \times 2 \rightarrow x = 20 \div 4 = 5$
x equals to 5. Let's review the choices provided:
  A) $x + 4 \rightarrow 5 + 4 = 9$ 20 is not divisible by 9.
  B) $2x - 4 \rightarrow 2 \times 5 - 4 = 6$ 20 is not divisible by 6.
  C) $x - 2 \rightarrow 5 - 2 = 3$ 20 is not divisible by 3.
  D) $x \times 4 \rightarrow 5 \times 4 = 20$ 20 is divisible by 20.
  E) $x + 1 \rightarrow 5 + 1 = 6$ 20 is not divisible by 6.

The answer is D.

14) Choice C is correct

$\frac{1}{8} = 0.125 \rightarrow C = 5$, $\frac{1}{20} = 0.05 \rightarrow D = 5 \rightarrow C \times D = 5 \times 5 = 25$

15) Choice C is correct

Use cross product to solve for x. $\frac{x}{x-3} = \frac{4}{5} \rightarrow 5 \times x = 4 \times (x - 3) \rightarrow 5x = 4x - 12 \rightarrow x = -12$

$\rightarrow x - 5 = -12 - 5 = -17$

16) Choice C is correct

x is the number of all sales profit and 2% of it is: $2\% \times x = 0.02x$, Employee's revenue:

$$0.02x + 4,000$$

17) Choice B is correct

Number of biology book: 35, total number of books; $35 + 95 + 80 = 210$

the ratio of the number of biology books to the total number of books is: $\dfrac{35}{210} = \dfrac{1}{6}$

18) Choice C is correct.

$6,000 + A - 200 = 7,400 \rightarrow 6,000 + A = 7,400 + 200 = 7,600 \rightarrow A = 7,600 - 6,000 = 1,600$

19) Choice D is correct

Let x be all expenses, then $\dfrac{22}{100}x = \$660 \;\rightarrow\; x = \dfrac{100 \times \$660}{22} = \$3,000$

Mr. Jones spent for his rent: $\dfrac{27}{100} \times \$3,000 = \$810$

20) Choice C is correct

$5 \times M + 4 = 5 \rightarrow 5 \times M = 5 - 4 = 1 \rightarrow M = \dfrac{1}{5}$

21) Choice E is correct

$\dfrac{42.6}{100} = 0.426$

22) Choice B is correct

The angles on a straight line add up to 180 degrees. Then: $x + 25 + y + 2x + y = 180$

Then, $3x + 2y = 180 - 25 \rightarrow 3(35) + 2y = 155, \rightarrow 2y = 155 - 105 = 50 \rightarrow y = 25$

23) Choice B is correct

let x be the number of gallons of water the container holds when it is full.

Then; $\dfrac{7}{24}x = 3.5 \rightarrow x = \dfrac{24 \times 3.5}{7} = 12$

24) Choice C is correct.

The ratio of lions to tigers is 5 to 3 at the zoo. Therefore, total number of lions and tigers must be divisible by 8. $5 + 3 = 8$, From the numbers provided, only 98 is not divisible by 8.

25) Choice A is correct

If x is greater than 18, then $\dfrac{1}{6}$ of x must be greater than: $\dfrac{1}{6} \times 18 = 3$.

SSAT Middle Level Mathematics Practice Test 5 Section 1

1) Choice C is correct

Use distance formula: $Distance = Rate \times time \Rightarrow 420 = 50 \times T$, divide both sides by 50. $420 \div 50 = T \Rightarrow T = 8.4 \ hours$. Change hours to minutes for the decimal part. $0.4 \ hours = 0.4 \times 60 = 24 \ minutes$.

2) Choice B is correct

To find the discount, multiply the number by $(100\% - rate \ of \ discount)$.Therefore, for the first discount we get: $(D) (100\% - 20\%) = (D) (0.80) = 0.80 \ D$

For increase of 10%: $(0.80 \ D) (100\% + 10\%) = (0.80 \ D) (1.10) = 0.88 \ D = \ 88\% \ of \ D$

3) Choice A is correct

0.55 equals $55M$. Then:$0.55 = 55M \rightarrow M = \frac{0.55}{55} = 0.01$

4) Choice B is correct

Use simple interest formula:$I = prt$,(I = interest, p = principal, r = rate, t = time)

t is for one year. For 3 months, t is $\frac{1}{4}$ or 0.25. $I = (4,800)(0.05)(0.25) = 60$

5) Choice A is correct

Three times a certain number, increased by 12, is equal to 39. Write an equation and solve.

$3x + 12 = 39 \rightarrow 3x = 39 - 12 = 27 \rightarrow x = \dfrac{27}{3} = 9$

6) Choice A is correct

30 percent of a number is 150. Therefore, the number is 500. $0.30x = 150 \rightarrow x = \frac{150}{0.30} = 500$

12 percent of 500 is 75. $0.12 \times 500 = 60$

7) Choice E is correct

$average = \dfrac{sum \ of \ terms}{number \ of \ terms} \Rightarrow 18 = \dfrac{13 + 15 + 20 + x}{4} \Rightarrow 72 = 48 + x \Rightarrow x = 24$

8) Choice C is correct

Add the first 5 numbers. $40 + 45 + 50 + 35 + 55 = 225$

To find the distance traveled in the next 5 hours, multiply the average by number of hours.

$Distance = Average \times Rate = 50 \times 5 = 250$, Add both numbers. $250 + 225 = 475$

9) Choice C is correct

John has N toy cars. Jack has 4 more cars than John. Therefore, Jack has $N + 4$ toy cars. Jack gives John 3 cars. Now, Jack has $(N + 4 - 3)\ N + 1$ toy cars.

10) Choice C is correct

$$\frac{x + 4}{5} = 2 \rightarrow x + 4 = 2 \times 5 = 10 \rightarrow x = 10 - 4 = 6$$

11) Choice E is correct

Th ratio of boy to girls is $2 : 3$. Therefore, there are 2 boys out of 5 students. To find the answer, first divide the total number of students by 5, then multiply the result by 2.

$$600 \div 5 = 120 \Rightarrow 120 \times 2 = 240$$

12) Choice C is correct

Let x be the number. Write the equation and solve for x.

$\frac{2}{3} \times 18 = \frac{2}{5} \cdot x \Rightarrow \frac{2 \times 18}{3} = \frac{2x}{5}$, use cross multiplication to solve for x.

$$5 \times 36 = 2x \times 3 \Rightarrow 180 = 6x \Rightarrow x = 30$$

13) Choice A is correct

One pound of cheese costs $0.96. *One pound* $= 16\ ounces$, 16 ounces of cheese costs $0.96. Then, 1 ounce of chees costs $(0.96 \div 16)$ $0.06. 6 ounces of cheese costs $(6 \times \$0.06)$ $0.36.

14) Choice D is correct

Write the equation and solve for B: $0.60A = 0.20B$, divide both sides by 0.20, then you will have $\frac{0.60}{0.20}A = B$, therefore: $B = 3A$, and B is 3 times of A or it's 300% of A.

15) Choice B is correct

$\frac{510}{600} = 0.85 = 85\%$. Therefore, the discount is: $100\% - 85\% = 15\%$

16) Choice D is correct

If 17 balls are removed from the bag at random, there will be one ball in the bag. The probability of choosing a brown ball is 1 out of 18. Therefore, the probability of not choosing a brown ball is 17 out of 18 and the probability of having not a brown ball after removing 17 balls is the same.

17) Choice C is correct

Let x be the number. Write the equation and solve for x. $(24 - x) \div x = 3$. Multiply both sides by x. $(24 - x) = 3x$, then add x both sides. $24 = 4x$, now divide both sides by 4. $x = 6$

18) Choice A is correct

The percent of girls playing tennis is: $40\% \times 25\% = 0.40 \times 0.25 = 0.10 = 10\%$

19) Choice D is correct

The failing rate is 11 out of $55 = \frac{11}{55}$. Change the fraction to percent: $\frac{11}{55} \times 100\% = 20\%$

20 percent of students failed. Therefore, 80 percent of students passed the exam.

20) Choice E is correct

$3x + 10 = 49 \rightarrow 3x = 49 - 10 = 39 \rightarrow x = \dfrac{39}{3} = 13$

21) Choice A is correct

$N \times \frac{4}{3} \times 5 = 0$, then N must be 0.

22) Choice E is correct

$12 is what percent of $48? $12 \div 48 = 0.25 = 25\%$

23) Choice E is correct

Let x be the number. Write the equation and solve for x.

$40\% \ of \ x = 8 \Rightarrow 0.40 \ x = 8 \Rightarrow x = 8 \div 0.40 = 20$

24) Choice E is correct

$\frac{z}{5} = 5 \rightarrow z = 5 \times 5 = 25, z + 3 = 25 + 3 = 28$

25) Choice A is correct

Let x be the number of years. Therefore, $2,000 per year equals $2000x$. starting from $28,000 annual salary means you should add that amount to $2000x$. Income more than that is:

$I > 2000x + 28000$

SSAT Middle Level Mathematics Practice Test 5 Section 2

1) Choice C is correct

Jacob has x dollars and he receives $150. Therefore, he has $x + 150$.

He then buys a bicycle that costs $120. Now, he has: $x + 150 - 120 = x + 30$

2) Choice A is correct

$$\frac{x-3}{8} + 4 = 20 \rightarrow \frac{x-3}{8} = 20 - 4 = 16 \rightarrow x - 3 = 16 \times 8 = 128 \rightarrow$$
$$x = 128 + 3 = 131$$

3) Choice E is correct

Ethan needs an 75% average to pass for five exams. Therefore, the sum of 5 exams must be at lease $5 \times 75 = 375$, The sum of 4 exams is: $68 + 72 + 85 + 90 = 315$.

The minimum score Jason can earn on his fifth and final test to pass is:$375 - 315 = 60$

4) Choice B is correct

The width of a rectangle is $6x$ and its length is $8x$. Then, the perimeter of the rectangle is $28x$.

Perimeter of a rectangle $= 2(width + length) = 2(6x + 8x) = 28x$

The perimeter of the rectangle is 56. Then:$28x = 56 \rightarrow x = 2$

5) Choice C is correct

Use simple interest formula: $I = prt$, (I = interest, p = principal, r = rate, t = time)

$I = (8,000)(0.045)(5) = 1,800$

6) Choice D is correct

$(9 - 5) \times 4 = 8 + \square$

Then:$4 \times 4 = 8 + \square$, $16 = 8 + \square$, then $\square = 8$

7) Choice C is correct

The distance between Jason and Joe is 9 miles. Jason running at 5.5 miles per hour and Joe is running at the speed of 7 miles per hour. Therefore, every hour the distance is 1.5 miles less.

$9 \div 1.5 = 6$

8) Choice E is correct

There are y tables that can each seat 5 people and there are x tables that can each seat 8 people. Therefore, $5y + 8x$ people can be seated in the classroom

9) Choice E is correct

The formula for the area of the circle is: $= \pi r^2$,

The area of the circle is 64 π. Therefore: $A = \pi r^2 \Rightarrow 64\pi = \pi r^2$, Divide both sides by π:

$64 = r^2 \Rightarrow r = 8$, Diameter of a circle is 2 $\times$ radius. Then: Diameter $= 2 \times 8 = 16$

10) Choice D is correct

To find the discount, multiply the number by $(100\% - rate\ of\ discount)$. Therefore, for the first discount we get: $(400)(100\% - 15\%) = (400)(0.85)$, For the next 15% discount: $(400)(0.85)(0.85)$

11) Choice D is correct

$$4 \div \frac{1}{6} = 24$$

12) Choice A is correct

The width of the rectangle is twice its length. Let x be the length. Then, $width = 2x$

Perimeter of the rectangle is $2\ (width + length) = 2(2x + x) = 60 \Rightarrow 6x = 60 \Rightarrow x = 10$

Length of the rectangle is 10 meters.

13) Choice C is correct

$$3x + 12 = 48 \rightarrow 3x = 48 - 12 = 36 \rightarrow x = \frac{36}{3} = 12$$

14) Choice C is correct

$$average\ (mean) = \frac{sum\ of\ terms}{number\ of\ terms} \Rightarrow 88 = \frac{sum\ of\ terms}{50} \Rightarrow sum = 88 \times 50 = 4400$$

The difference of 94 and 69 is 25. Therefore, 25 should be subtracted from the sum.

$$4400 - 25 = 4375, mean = \frac{sum\ of\ terms}{number\ of\ terms} \Rightarrow mean = \frac{4375}{50} = 87.5$$

15) Choice D is correct

$average = \frac{sum\ of\ terms}{number\ of\ terms} \Rightarrow$ (average of 6 numbers) $12 = \frac{sum\ of\ numbers}{6} \Rightarrow$ sum of 6 numbers is $12 \times 6 = 72$

(average of 4 numbers) $10 = \frac{sum\ of\ numbers}{4} \Rightarrow$ sum of 4 numbers is $10 \times 4 = 40$

$sum\ of\ 6\ numbers - sum\ of\ 4\ numbers = sum\ of\ 2\ numbers$

$72 - 40 = 32$ average of 2 numbers $= \frac{32}{2} = 16$

16) Choice B is correct

$x + 5 = 8 \rightarrow x = 8 - 5 = 3, 2y - 1 = 5 \rightarrow 2y = 6 \rightarrow y = 3, xy + 10 = 3 \times 3 + 10 = 19$

17) Choice B is correct

The probability of choosing a Hearts is $\frac{13}{52} = \frac{1}{4}$

18) Choice B is correct

From the choices provided, only $\frac{1}{2}$ is greater than $\frac{1}{5}$.

19) Choice A is correct

2,500 out of 65,000 equals to $\frac{2500}{55000} = \frac{25}{550} = \frac{1}{22}$

20) Choice D is correct

$3x - 4 = 23 \rightarrow 3x = 27 \rightarrow x = 9$, then $2x + 6 = 2 \times 9 + 6 = 18 + 6 = 24$

21) Choice C is correct

the population is increased by 15% and 20%. 15% increase changes the population to 115% of original population. For the second increase, multiply the result by 120%.

$(1.15) \times (1.20) = 1.38 = 138\%$, 38 percent of the population is increased after two years.

22) Choice A is correct

First, find the number. Let x be the number. Write the equation and solve for x.

150% of a number is 75, then: $1.5 \times x = 75 \Rightarrow x = 75 \div 1.5 = 50$

90% of 50 is: $0.9 \times 50 = 45$

23) Choice B is correct

Plug in 104 for F and then solve for C.

$$C = \frac{5}{9}(F - 32) \Rightarrow C = \frac{5}{9}(104 - 32) \Rightarrow C = \frac{5}{9}(72) = 40$$

24) Choice B is correct

The perimeter of the trapezoid is 36.

Therefore, the missing side (height) is $= 36 - 8 - 12 - 6 = 10$

Area of a trapezoid: $A = \frac{1}{2}h(b_1 + b_2) = \frac{1}{2}(10)(6 + 8) = 70$

25) Choice D is correct

If the length of the box is 27, then the width of the box is one third of it, 9, and the height of the box is 3 (one third of the width). The volume of the box is:

$Volume\ of\ a\ box = (length) \times (width) \times (height) = (27) \times (9) \times (3) = 729$

"Effortless Math Education" Publications

Effortless Math Education authors' team strives to prepare and publish the best quality Mathematics learning resources to make learning Math easier for all. We hope that our publications help you or your student learn Math in an effective way.

We all in Effortless Math wish you good luck and successful studies!

Effortless Math Authors

www.EffortlessMath.com

... So Much More Online!

✓ FREE Math lessons

✓ More Math learning books!

✓ Mathematics Worksheets

✓ Online Math Tutors

Need a PDF version of this book?

Please visit www.EffortlessMath.com

Made in the USA
Coppell, TX
13 November 2020